Dorothy Parker was ... to J. Henry and Elizabeth Rothschild on August 22, 1893. Parker's childhood was not a happy one. Her mother died young, and Dorothy did not enjoy a good relationship with her father and stepmother. She began her education at a Catholic convent school in Manhattan before being sent away to Miss Dana's Academy in Morristown, New Jersey. In 1916, Frank Crowninshield gave Parker an editorial position at *Vogue*, following its publication of a number of her poems. The next year she moved on to write for *Vanity Fair*, where she would later become the theater critic. That same year she met and married Edwin Pond Parker II, whom she divorced a few years later. It was at *Vanity Fair* that Parker met her associates with whom she would form the Algonquin Round Table, the famed New York literary circle. In 1925, Parker also began writing short stories for a new magazine called *The New Yorker*. Her relationship with that publication would last, off and on, until 1957. Parker went abroad in the 1930s, continuing to write poetry and stories. In Europe she met Alan Campbell, whom she married in 1934. The couple divorced in 1947 but remarried in 1950, remaining together until Campbell's death in 1963. Throughout this period in her life, Parker continued to publish collections of her work, including *Enough Rope* (1926), *Sunset Gun* (1928), *Laments for the Living* (1930), and *Death and Taxes* (1931). Her last great work was a play, *The Ladies of the Corridor*, which she wrote with Arnaud d'Usseau, published in 1954. Parker died on June 7, 1967.

Colleen Breese teaches in the English Department at the University of Toledo, and is the author of *Excuse My Dust: The Art of Dorothy Parker's Serious Fiction*, and editor of *Dorothy Parker: Complete Stories* for Viking/Penguin. She resides with her family in Sylvania, Ohio.

DOROTHY PARKER

COMPLETE POEMS

WITH AN INTRODUCTION
BY COLLEEN BREESE

PENGUIN BOOKS

PENGUIN BOOKS

Published by the Penguin Group
Penguin Putnam Inc., 375 Hudson Street,
New York, New York 10014, U.S.A.
Penguin Books Ltd, 27 Wrights Lane, London W8 5TZ, England
Penguin Books Australia Ltd, Ringwood, Victoria, Australia
Penguin Books Canada Ltd, 10 Alcorn Avenue,
Toronto, Ontario, Canada M4V 3B2
Penguin Books (N.Z.) Ltd, 182–190 Wairau Road, Auckland 10, New Zealand

Penguin Books Ltd, Registered Offices:
Harmondsworth, Middlesex, England

First published in Penguin Books 1999

3 5 7 9 10 8 6 4 2

The selections in this book appeared in *The Bookman, Life, McCall's, The Nation, The New Republic, New York Herald Tribune, New York World, The New Yorker, The Saturday Evening Post, Saturday Review, Vanity Fair, Vogue, The Yale Review,* and in Dorothy Parker's *Enough Rope* (1926), *Sunset Gun* (1928) *Death and Taxes* (1931), *Not So Deep as a Well* (1936), and *The Portable Dorothy Parker* (1944), published by The Viking Press.
"Letter to Robert Benchley" courtesy of the Department of Special Collection, Mugar Memorial Library, Boston University.
"Ballade of Understandable Ambitions," "Song of a Contented Heart," "Song of the Wilderness," "A Triolet," "Paean," "Song [3]," "And Oblige," and "Triolet [2]" published in *The Saturday Evening Post.* Copyright 1923 The Saturday Evening Post; copyright renewed 1950. Used by permission.

LIBRARY OF CONGRESS CATALOGING IN PUBLICATION DATA
Parker, Dorothy, 1893–1967.
[Poems]
Complete poems/Dorothy Parker: with an introduction by Colleen Breese.
p. cm.—(Penguin twentieth-century classics)
Includes bibliographical references.
ISBN 0 14 11.8022 6
I. Breese, Colleen. II. Title. III. Series.
PS3531.A5855A17 1999
811'.52—dc21 98-47392

Printed in the United States of America
Set in Stemple Garamond

CONTENTS

INTRODUCTION

Dorothy Parker was her own worst critic. "I want so much to write well, though I know I don't, and that I didn't make it. But during and at the end of my life, I will adore those who have," she remarked to an interviewer in 1956, when her reputation as master of light verse had already been firmly established for thirty years.

In 1926, Parker made publishing history with the publication of her best-selling collection of poems, *Enough Rope*. Her spicy verbal wit gained acclaim, as well: She perpetrated such puns as "You can lead a horticulture, but you can't make her think" and once commented about a friend who had returned from England with a broken leg, "She probably got it sliding down a barrister." But it is her poetry and fiction that established the literary phenomenon known as Dorothy Parker, who really did "make it."

What she made was something new the era craved, and her distinctive voice became part of its lively cultural conversation. More opportunities for writers existed in the first decade of the twentieth century than perhaps ever before or since in the history of American letters. In those days before the dominance of radio, film, and television, the written word was paramount, and newspapers and magazines flourished. The boroughs of New York City alone published twenty-five daily newspapers, and literary magazines were at their zenith. This world of mass commercial publishing became Parker's milieu. Her audience was broad in scope: there were the everyday readers who subscribed to the leading magazines and went to the theater; there were the cosmopolitans of New York who read its papers; and then there were the glittering literati who relished each other's work.

Parker's readership grew to include the sophisticates of the 1920s and 1930s who read Harold Ross's *New Yorker* magazine.

The era spanning the last decade of the nineteenth century and the first two decades of the twentieth was also a time of large-scale political movements and social changes among women. A new generation of women writers emerged. These "New Women," as Henry James labeled them, were concerned with winning women the rights that had been reserved for the male population: the vote, education, economic freedom, access to professions and careers, a public voice, and public power. They were educated and progressive; making a clean break with the past, they carved out new identities and in a sense created themselves. Women writers of the era did not feel bound to marry and have children as their life's work. Rejecting the traditional "women's sphere," they claimed for themselves the "male territory" of art. Many were fiercely determined not to be thought of merely as "women writers," and felt it necessary to distance themselves from other women. Gender was not part of the definition of who one was.

Born into this tradition, Dorothy Parker, née Rothschild, said that her most fervent prayer had been "Please, God, don't let me write like a woman."

Dorothy Rothschild was born prematurely on August 22, 1893, at her family's vacation home in the affluent summer resort of West End, New Jersey, and spent most of her life in New York City. Biographers disagree about her education, but the most reliable and carefully researched source, Marion Meade's *Dorothy Parker: What Fresh Hell Is This?*, contends that Dorothy's formal education ended "abruptly and inexplicably" in 1908, when she was fourteen. Parker says that she merely "fell into writing . . . being one of those awful children who wrote verses." She began her professional life in 1915 when, at age twenty-two and orphaned, she went to work as a caption writer for *Vogue* at a salary of ten dollars a week. By 1917 she had transferred to *Van-*

ity Fair, Vogue's sister magazine, and worked until 1920 for editor Frank Crowninshield. In 1918 she replaced P. G. Wodehouse as drama reviewer and became New York's only woman drama critic, a job from which she was fired in 1920 for outspoken criticism. What makes Parker's early drama reviewing so interesting is her rejection of the prevailing standards for female writing and thinking; she presented herself not so much "as a bad girl," Meade says, "but as a bad boy, a firecracker who was aggressively proud of being tough, quirky, feisty."

On June 30, 1917, Dorothy married Edwin Pond Parker II, of Hartford, Connecticut, the son and grandson of prominent Congregational clergymen. Dorothy, in taking Parker's name, denied the Jewish heritage of her father for the rest of her life. Her mother had been born to a successful British-American family of skilled gunsmiths. Dorothy had attended a private Catholic girls school in New York City, Blessed Sacrament Academy (where she jokingly referred to the Immaculate Conception as "spontaneous combustion"), and later went to Miss Dana's Academy, a restricted Protestant boarding school in Morristown, New Jersey. Hinting at her background, Parker always referred to herself as a "mongrel."

After World War I, New York became an especially heady place in which to live and write. In June 1919, Parker and her fellow literary wits initiated the famous Round Table at Frank Case's Algonquin Hotel, where they met daily to exchange insults and eat lunch. The charter *illuminati* of this "Vicious Circle," whose wit tended to be caustic, urbane, and neurotic, included the *New York Times* journalists Alexander Woollcott (the drama critic) and George S. Kaufman, later a Pulitzer Prize–winning playwright; Heywood Broun from the *New York Tribune*; Franklin Pierce Adams (F.P.A.) from the *New York World*; Marc Connelly from the *New York Morning Telegraph*, also a Pulitzer-winning playwright, and a collaborator of Kaufman; the theatrical press agent John Peter Toohey; the writers Robert Benchley and Robert Sherwood; and Harold Ross, the founder of *The New Yorker*. Dorothy Parker was the only female in the group, and none of them could have predicted that she would become the best writer of the lot.

The habitués of the Round Table depended upon the appreciation of a fairly literate readership. They gained their notoriety by keeping their tongues honed sharper than the knives at the table, and their mastery of the putdown became legendary. When Noel Coward commented on Edna Ferber's mannish suit and hairdo, telling her, "You look almost like a man," she replied, "So do you." A young man who bragged to Parker that he couldn't bear fools was promptly told, "That's queer. Your mother could." When told that Clare Boothe Luce, whose pretentiousness Parker couldn't abide, was always kind to inferiors, Parker, in puzzlement, asked, "Where does she find them?"

When her husband Eddie returned to New York after the war, Dorothy's interest in him decreased. Their interest in alcohol, however, increased. Eddie, never an intellectual heavyweight, was a fish out of water among the Algonquinites; their verbal wit and putdowns only made him feel more insecure, a circumstance that Dorothy did little to help. Instead, she often humiliated him in public by telling stories that portrayed him as the hapless victim. They separated in 1924 and finally divorced in 1928.

From 1919 to 1923, Parker wrote poems, sketches, essays, and columns for more than thirty-five different literary journals and magazines; these pieces represent her apprenticeship as a professional writer. In many of her early magazine pieces can be seen the seeds of what would later be expanded and developed into the Parkerian formula for short stories and epigrammatic poetry. Throughout the 1920s and 1930s, Parker contributed to such diverse magazines as *The Saturday Evening Post*, *McCall's*, *Ladies' Home Journal*, *Ainslee's*, *Everybody's*, *Life*, and after its shaky beginning in 1925, *The New Yorker*.

Parker's first poem, "Any Porch," published in *Vanity Fair* in September 1915, is an uneven attempt at presenting nine different female voices who discuss such various topics as the vote for women, a game of bridge, Irene Castle's bobbed hair, and the war in France. Four poems, also of little merit, followed in the same magazine in 1916. The next year witnessed her series of "hate songs," compact satiric descriptions of husbands and wives, actors and actresses, bores, relatives, slackers, and the like. These made Parker very popular. Sharpening her talent for light verse, she soon began to build a reputation as a sophisticated young writer with a witty message. For example, at the time Freud was becoming popular in American intellectual circles, she concocted "The Passionate Freudian to His Love" (1921), which relies on several puns and shows not only a much-matured poet but also Parker's epigrammatic wit:

> So come dwell a while on that distant isle
> In the brilliant tropic weather;
> Where a Freud in need is a Freud indeed,
> We'll be always Jung together.

By the time her first collection of poems, *Enough Rope,* was published in 1926, her reputation as "the wittiest woman in America"—a reputation encouraged by frequent mention in F.P.A.'s *World* column—was firmly in place. Parker soon played a distinctive role in the chorus of female literary voices calling for equality and social independence for women. She was keenly aware of the struggles and changes in women's lives around her. Her "little woman" point of view, a literary voice with a tough edge to it, would serve her throughout her career, whether she was writing drama, short fiction, drama or book reviews, or poems. In her verse she specialized in the hard truths, particularly truths about death—death in love, death in life, and death in dying. For example, in "Unfortunate Coincidence" (1926) she wrote, with tongue in cheek:

> By the time you swear you're his,
> Shivering and sighing,
> And he vows his passion is
> Infinite, undying—

> Lady, make a note of this:
>   One of you is lying.

In "Experience" (1926), the speaker glibly admonishes the inexperienced to understand that love does not run a smooth course:

> Some men break your heart in two,
>   Some men fawn and flatter,
> Some men never look at you;
>   And that cleans up the matter.

In the dark years of her youth, depressed, unhappy in love, and alcoholic, Parker attempted suicide four times. Suicide is a recurrent theme in her poetry and fiction, most notably in the award-winning story, "Big Blonde" (1929). One of her best-known poems, "Résumé" (1925), displays a side of Parker's wit that is largely autobiographical and best described as black humor:

> Razors pain you;
> Rivers are damp;
> Acids stain you;
> And drugs cause cramp.
> Guns aren't lawful;
> Nooses give;
> Gas smells awful;
> You might as well live.

In "Rhyme Against Living" (1926), composed after her second suicide attempt, Parker again darkly rails against life:

> If wild my breast and sore my pride,
> I bask in dreams of suicide;
> If cool my heart and high my head,
> I think, "How lucky are the dead!"

Early on, Parker had decided that life was not fair. Casting a cynical eye upon the things expected to give pleasure and reward—art, love, work, rest—in "Coda" (1928), she argues that there is not much worth living for; she again morbidly contemplates suicide:

> There's little in taking or giving,
>   There's little in water or wine;
> This living, this living, this living,
>   Was never a project of mine.
> Oh, hard is the struggle, and sparse is
>   The gain of the one at the top,
> For art is a form of catharsis,
>   And love is a permanent flop,
> And work is the province of cattle,
>   And rest's for a clam in a shell,
> So I'm thinking of throwing the battle—
>   Would you kindly direct me to hell?

Her many unhappy love affairs led to a jaded view of men:

> They hail you as their morning star
> Because you are the way you are.
> If you return the sentiment,
> They'll try to make you different;
> And once they have you, safe and sound,
> They want to change you all around.
> Your moods and ways they put a curse on;
> They'd make of you another person.
> They cannot let you go your gait;
> They influence and educate.
> They'd alter all that they admired.
> They make me sick, they make me tired.

("Men," 1926)

The speakers in her poems are mainly urban sophisticates, and her pages are fraught with images of isolation, degradation, loneliness, and depression; everything Parker touched is transformed by her narrative idiom. No matter the situation she describes, she involves readers, makes them listen to the peculiarly American and utterly contemporary voices of her speakers and narrators. It is her style, her art, her many-sided humor, her irony, her sarcasm, her tenderness, her pathos that readers pay attention to, as in "The False Friends" (1926):

> They laid their hands upon my head,
> They stroked my cheek and brow;
> And time could heal a hurt, they said,
> And time could dim a vow.
>
> And they were pitiful and mild
> Who whispered to me then,
> "The heart that breaks in April, child,
> Will mend in May again."
>
> Oh, many a mended heart they knew.
> So old they were, and wise.
> And little did they have to do
> To come to me with lies!
>
> Who flings me silly talk of May
> Shall meet a bitter soul;
> For June was nearly spent away
> Before my heart was whole.

Parker's attitude toward human folly was satiric; her poems mock and undermine as they unfold through repetitions that underscore and heighten her satirical intent. By making readers pay attention to who is speaking and what the implications of these messages are, Parker forces readers to read behind and between the lines of her deceptively simple situations and messages in order to appreciate fully and understand her art. "The purpose of the writer is to say what he feels and sees," Parker insisted. "Those who write fantasies" she did not consider artists.

During the 1920s, throughout Prohibition, Parker continued to drink at New York speakeasies. And she continued to fall in and out of love. In November 1922, after a torrid affair with Charlie MacArthur, Dorothy had a legal hospital abortion. This was soon followed by her first suicide attempt. Depressed, but ever the wit, Dorothy said it served her right for putting all her eggs in one bastard. The first poem published after the abortion, "One Perfect Rose," appeared in *Life* on January 24, 1923. In this classic, hyperbolic, and very funny poem, Parker takes to task the young lover who doesn't know that his symbolic expression of love is seen as cheap. In the final lines, the sarcastic and frustrated speaker turns the romantic symbol, the "one perfect rose," into a term of both derision and hilarity:

> A single flow'r he sent me, since we met.
>   All tenderly his messenger he chose;
> Deep-hearted, pure, with scented dew still wet—
>   One perfect rose.
>
> I knew the language of the floweret;
>   "My fragile leaves," it said, "his heart enclose."
> Love long has taken for his amulet
>   One perfect rose.
>
> Why is it no one ever sent me yet
>   One perfect limousine, do you suppose?
> Ah no, it's always just my luck to get
>   One perfect rose.

Here is Parker at her best, in the full bloom of maturity as an epigrammatic poet, even as her personal life is collapsing around her. Her romantic disasters continued with a succession of charming men until her marriage to Alan Campbell, a personable young actor and writer, in 1934. This on-again-off-again marriage lasted until his untimely death, at age fifty-nine, in 1963. Campbell collaborated with Parker during the 1930s and 1940s, when they spent much of their time in Hollywood writing screenplays. The highlight of their movie-writing career occurred in 1937, when they were both nominated for an Academy Award for their original screenplay *A Star Is Born*. Dorothy was nominated again ten years later for her work on *Smash Up: The Story of a Woman*, starring Susan Hayward, who was also nominated as best actress.

After her marriage to Campbell, she would write only three more poems. Her last, "War Song," appeared in *The New Yorker* on March 4, 1944, four months after her short story "The Lovely Leave" was published in December 1943. Both works reflect her experiences with Campbell, who served in World War II. On October 21, 1953, her feminist play *The Ladies of the Corridor*, written with Arnaud d'Usseau, opened on Broadway with a cast that included Betty Field and Walter Matthau. Most New York critics gave the play favorable reviews; George Jean Nathan voted it the best American play in Drama Circle balloting. Nevertheless, it closed in six weeks. Her final story appeared in 1958; between 1957 and 1963 she returned to reviewing books, this time for *Esquire* magazine.

On April 30, 1958, Parker received the Marjorie Peabody Waite Award from the National Institute of Arts and Letters. At the awards ceremony, Malcolm Cowley, president of the institute, read a citation by Parker's good friend Lillian Hellman:

TO DOROTHY PARKER, born in West End, New Jersey, because the clean wit of her verse and the sharp perception in her stories have produced a brilliant record of our time. Because Miss Parker has a true talent, even her early work gives us as much pleasure as it did thirty years ago.

That same year, Parker was also honored with an artist-in-residency at Yaddo, a retreat for artists, writers, and composers near Saratoga Springs, New York. The following year, Parker was elected a member of the National Institute.

Now, nearly three-quarters of a century after Parker's first book of poems was published, this volume finally collects all of her poems. Parker left not only a rich legacy to American letters, theater, and film, but an enormous oeuvre as well; her total output has been largely uncollected and unrecognized. That she had a profound influence on American literature, especially on the short story and epigrammatic poetry, is without question. As serious art, Parker's work deserves serious critical attention. Yet critics have chosen to focus primarily on her life rather than on her literary legacy. Also without question is the fact that she was a woman ahead of her time—a female rebel, yet "one of the boys"—and as such she addresses a very important part of American women's history. It is therefore necessary to view Parker's works in the context of the times in which they were written, in order to determine how accurately they comment on the issues of her day as well as our own.

While suffrage had quickened the trend toward equality under the law, discrimination against women still persisted in all realms, and women were struggling against restrictions throughout the 1920s and 1930s. For example, several states still denied women the right to serve on juries well into the 1940s. Women had failed to achieve political equality. Economic advances, too, were minimal. Although women had substantially increased sexual equality, shifts in manners and morals did not interfere with the perpetuation of a sexual division of labor. A social revolution was required in the way men and women thought of each other and in the distribution of responsibilities within marriage and the family. But discrimination in family responsibilities, and in education, salaries, and promotions, remained abundant in the 1920s. The gains women had made in the career world during the 1920s began to be lost around 1930, and during the Depression a renewed emphasis on homemaking wielded a crushing blow to feminist hopes for equality.

The notion, commonly held even now, that women were sexually active but politically apathetic during the 1920s has created for them a sexually stereotyped historical role. But Parker's work, we see today, points a sharp finger at the stereotype, and defies it. She keenly attests to the legal, economic, social, and emotional restrictions on women's lives and to their ongoing, frequently frustrated struggles to break free. Her poems give weary witness to the throes of revolution.

Her major themes are not only a window into the 1920s and 1930s but also remain universal and timeless in their relevancy to topics of the present day: lack of communication between women and men, disintegration of relationships, jealousy, alcoholism, motherhood, human frailties, inane social conventions, the affectations and hypocrisies of a patriarchal society, women's emotional dependency upon men, the selfishness of the wealthy, and the danger of emptiness in women's lives. The targets of her satire are timeless too: the upper class, the self-pitying, the shallow and boring, the envious, the egotistical and egocentric, the depraved, the bigoted, and the jealous. Her poetic devices are of venerable origins and yet still fresh and vital: satire, irony, pathos, tragedy, paradox, sentiment, repetition, exaggeration, sarcasm, dialogue, monologue, narrative, clichéd speech, humor, and scalding, unforgettable wit. The hallmarks of Parker's poems—sympathy and compassion, compression, impeccable grammar and syntax, outstanding diction, double voices and double consciousness, feminism, criticism and self-criticism, subversion and subtext, reversal, and dissection of social manners—point not only to the seriousness and quality of Dorothy Parker's work, but also to its importance as timeless social commentary and as insight about women and men.

That Parker was a feminist is also undeniable; her voice is confined for the most part to women and what was important to them, yet her speakers do not talk about the home—in a time when the home was often their only choice. Parker places women in classic female situations, then subverts them; her satire occurs because we recognize the futility of the situation, not that of the speaker. In 1922 Thomas Masson said that Parker had suddenly found herself placed in a world that she "didn't like" and chose a "method of self-defense." Perhaps she did, but her enormous sympathy, her extraordinary talent, and her innate capacity for human emotions allowed her to voice and expose the sham and hypocrisy of mentally and morally bankrupt people, especially women. Her instinct for exposure has often resulted in her being called a cynic, but this label too is a false one, because Parker wrote satire, satire that attacks class consciousness, conspicuous consumption, the idle pursuit of pleasure, the self-absorbed (especially the female snob), the smug, the pretentious, the pathetic, the self-pitying, and even the self-victimized. Wyatt Cooper noted that Parker "didn't hit anybody who wasn't as big as she was, and she never picked unworthy targets." Her poems show a deeply concerned social conscience.

Parker wrote in a genre where imitators have fallen short of her example; she made no effort to keep alive her early reputation as a wit, and preferred to be called a satirist, never a humorist. "I don't want to be classed as a humorist," she said. "It makes me feel guilty. I've never read a good tough quotable female humorist, and I never was one myself. I couldn't do it." But satire was "another matter. They're the big boys. If I'd been called a satirist there'd be no living with me." Being called a "smartcracker" made her "sick and unhappy," as she saw "a hell of a distance between wisecracking and wit. Wit has truth in it; wisecracking is simply calisthenics with words."

Because she was a genius, she was a rarity. The power of her truth was focused on the conventional, the everyday, the neglected—and the texture of women's lives. For Parker the personal was painful and crippling, yet her perspective on human behavior transcends a particular moment to pass a psychological test of time. Her art was a highly personal art, an autonomous talent, not an alienated artifact of culture or legend; her creativity transcended her notoriety. She was a rebel working in a male-dominated literary tradition, and her humanism took oppression, particularly female oppression, as its most common subject. But she went further, portraying oppression on the basis of class, race, and politics. Her legacy can best be summed up as serious art, uniquely Dorothy Parker's, and for this it is best to let Parker have the last word.

> And let her loves, when she is dead,
>   Write this above her bones:
> "No more she lives to give us bread
>   Who asked her only stones."

("For a Sad Lady," 1926)

SUGGESTIONS FOR FURTHER READING

CRITICISM

Bunkers, Suzanne L. " 'I Am Outraged Womanhood': Dorothy Parker as Feminist and Social Critic." *Regionalism and the Female Imagination* 4 (1978): 25–35.

Douglas, George. *Women of the Twenties.* New York: Saybrook, 1989.

Gray, James. "Dream of Unfair Women: Nancy Hale, Clare Boothe Luce, and Dorothy Parker." In James Gray, *On Second Thought.* Minneapolis: University of Minnesota Press, 1946.

Hagopian, John. "You Were Perfectly Fine." *Insight I: Analyses of American Literature.* Frankfurt: A. M. Hirschgraben, 1962.

Labrie, Ross. "Dorothy Parker Revisited." *Canadian Review of American Studies* 7 (1976): 48–56.

Kinney, Arthur F. *Dorothy Parker.* Boston: Twayne, 1978.

Miller, Nina. "Making Love Modern: Dorothy Parker and Her Public." *American Literature* 64, no. 4 (1992): 763–784.

Shanahan, William. "Robert Benchley and Dorothy Parker: Punch and Judy in Formal Dress." *Rendezvous* 3, no. 1 (1968): 23–34.

Toth, Emily. "Dorothy Parker, Erica Jong, and New Feminist Humor." *Regionalism and the Female Imagination* 2, no. 2 (1977): 70–85.

Trichler, Paula A. "Verbal Subversions in Dorothy Parker: 'Trapped Like a Trap in a Trap.' " *Language and Style: An International Journal* 13, no. 4 (1980): 46–61.

Walker, Nancy. "Fragile and Dumb: The 'Little Woman' in Woman's Humor, 1900–1940." *Thalia: Studies in Literary Humor* 5 (1982), no. 2: 24–49.

Yates, Norris. "Dorothy Parker's Idle Men and Women." In Norris Wilson Yates, *The American Humorist: Conscience of the Twentieth Century.* Ames: Iowa State University Press, 1964.

BACKGROUND

Capron, Marion. "Dorothy Parker." *Writers at Work: The Paris Review Interviews.* Edited by Malcolm Cowley. New York: Viking, 1957. Reprinted in *Women Writers at Work.* Edited by George Plimpton. New York: Penguin, 1989.

Case, Frank. *Tales of a Wayward Inn.* New York: Frederick A. Stokes, 1938.

Douglas, Ann. *Terrible Honesty: Mongrel Manhattan in the 1920s.* New York: Farrar, Straus & Giroux, 1995.

Drennan, Robert, ed. *The Algonquin Wits.* New York: Citadel Press, 1968.

Gaines, James R. *Wit's End: Days and Nights of the Algonquin Round Table.* New York: Harcourt, 1977.

Grant, Jane. *Ross, The New Yorker, and Me.* New York: Raynel & Morrow, 1968.

Harriman, Margaret Case. *The Vicious Circle: The Story of the Algonquin Round Table.* New York: Harcourt, 1977.

Kramer, Dale. *Ross and The New Yorker.* New York: Doubleday, 1951.

Kunkel, Thomas. *Genius at Work: Harold Ross of The New Yorker.* New York: Random House, 1995.

DOROTHY PARKER BIOGRAPHIES

Frewin, Leslie. *The Late Mrs. Dorothy Parker.* New York: Macmillan, 1986.

Keats, John. *You Might As Well Live: The Life and Times of Dorothy Parker.* New York: Simon & Schuster, 1970.

Meade, Marion. *Dorothy Parker: What Fresh Hell Is This?* New York: Villard Books, 1988.

ANTHOLOGY

The Viking Portable Library: Dorothy Parker. New York:
Viking, 1944. Republished as *The Indispensable Dorothy
Parker.* New York: Book Society, 1944. Published again as *Se-
lected Short Stories.* New York: Editions for the Armed Ser-
vices, 1944. Revised and enlarged as *The Portable Dorothy
Parker.* New York: Viking, 1973; revised, 1976. Republished
as *The Collected Dorothy Parker.* London: Duckworth, 1973.

1893   August 22: Born in West End, New Jersey, to J. Henry Rothschild (a coat manufacturer) and Eliza A. (Marston) Rothschild (a schoolteacher).

1897   July 20: Mother dies.

1900–1908   Student at Blessed Sacrament Academy, New York City, and Miss Dana's Academy, Morristown, New Jersey. Formal education ends abruptly at age fourteen.

1913   December 28: Father dies.

1914   September: First published poem for money ($12), "Any Porch," *Vanity Fair*.

1915   First job, at *Vogue;* light verse published by Franklin P. Adams (F.P.A.).

1917–1920   Staff writer for *Vanity Fair*; April 1918–March 1920: replaces P. G. Wodehouse as drama reviewer.

1917   June 30: Marries Edwin Pond Parker II, of Hartford, Connecticut, descendant of prominent Congregational-clergy family.

1919   June: Round Table meets for the first time.

1920   January: Fired from *Vanity Fair* for outspoken criticism. Named drama reviewer for *Ainslee's* (May

1920–July 1923). Contributes freelance verse and prose to *Life*. Writes *High Society* with Frank Crowninshield and George S. Chappell.

1920–1923 Contributes essays and verse to *Saturday Evening Post*, *Ladies' Home Journal*, *Everybody's*, and *Life*.

1922 Writes song for "No Siree!" and acts in the production; writes *Nero* with Robert Benchley for *The 49ers*. Publishes first book, *Women I'm Not Married To; Men I'm Not Married To* (with F.P.A.). Fall: Has abortion.

1923 January: First suicide attempt.

1924 December 1: Play, *Close Harmony* (written with Elmer Rice) opens.

1925 Collaborates on novel, *Bobbed Hair* (serialized in *Collier's*, her chapter on January 17). First film script, *Business Is Business* (with George S. Kaufman).

1926 *Enough Rope* (poems) makes publishing history by becoming a best seller; first European trip. Second suicide attempt.

1927 October 1–March 1931: Book reviewer for the *New Yorker* as "Constant Reader"; also contributes fiction and poems. August 11, marches against execution of Sacco and Vanzetti in Boston.

1928 March 31: Divorces Eddie Parker. *Sunset Gun* (collected poems), another best seller; column for *McCall's*.

1929   "Big Blonde" wins O. Henry Award as year's best short story; second European trip.

1930   *Laments for the Living* (collected fiction); third suicide attempt; third European trip.

1931   *Death and Taxes* (collected poems); contributes drama reviews to the *New Yorker* and lyrics to *Shoot the Works* by Heywood Broun. On three-month contract for MGM in Hollywood.

1932   Fourth suicide attempt; fourth European trip.

1933   *After Such Pleasures* (collected stories) published.

1934   June 18: Marries Alan Campbell. Contributes to dialogue of *Here Is My Heart* and *One Hour Late* (both Paramount). Helps organize Screen Writers Guild.

1935   Contributes to dialogue of *Mary Burns, Fugitive*; to screenplay construction of *Hands Across the Table*; and to treatment of *Paris in Spring* (all Paramount); lyrics of *Big Broadcast of 1936* (Paramount).

1936   *Not So Deep as a Well* (collected poems); joint screenplay, *Three Married Men* and *Lady, Be Careful* (both Paramount) and *Suzy* (MGM); additional dialogue, *The Moon's Our Home* (Paramount). June: Helps found the Anti-Nazi league.

1937   Joint screenplay, *A Star Is Born*, for David Selznick; *Woman Chases Man* (United Artists). Fifth trip to Europe; reports on Loyalist cause from Spain for *New Masses*.

1938   Joint screenplay, *Sweethearts* (MGM); *Trade Winds* (United Artists).

1939   *Here Lies* (collected stories) published. Sixth trip to Europe.

1941   Joint screenplay, *Weekend for Three*; additional scenes and dialogue, *The Little Foxes* (both RKO).

1942   *Collected Stories*; joint original screenplay, *Saboteur* (Universal).

1944   *The Viking Portable Dorothy Parker*, poems and stories chosen by Parker.

1947   Joint original story, *Smash Up: The Story of a Woman* (Universal-International). Nominated for an Academy Award for best original screenplay. May 27: Divorced from Campbell.

1949   Joint screenplay, *The Fan* (20th Century-Fox); *The Coast of Illyria* (play, with Ross Evans) had three-week run in Dallas. Blacklisted in Hollywood.

1950   Remarries Alan Campbell; her story "Horsie" a basis for *Queen for a Day* (United Artists).

1952–1953   Testimony given against her before the House Un-American Activities Committee.

1953   *The Ladies of the Corridor* (play, written with Arnaud D'Usseau).

1955   Called before New York State joint legislative committee; pleads First Amendment.

1956   Lyrics to a song for *Candide* (musical).

1957–1963   Book reviewer for *Esquire;* 46 columns, 208 books reviewed.

1958   Receives Marjorie Peabody Waite Award, National Institute of Arts and Letters. Publishes last short story, "Bolt Behind the Blue," in December *Esquire*.

1959   Inducted into National Institute of Arts and Letters.

1963   June 14, Alan Campbell dies, apparent suicide, age 59.

1963–1964   Distinguished Visiting Professor of English, California State College at Los Angeles.

1964   Records stories and poems for Spoken Arts, Verve; publishes final magazine piece in December *Esquire*.

1965   *Short Story* anthology, coedited with Frederick B. Shroyer.

1967   June 7: Discovered dead, of a heart attack, in her room at Hotel Volney, New York City, almost 75 years old.

1993   August 22: United States Postal Service issues commemorative Dorothy Parker stamp in West End, New Jersey, as the tenth issue in its Literary Arts Series, which began in 1979 and includes many other famous American authors.

A NOTE ON THE TEXT

The poems that appear here are faithfully reproduced from Dorothy Parker's original collections: *Enough Rope* (1926); *Sunset Gun* (1928); *Death and Taxes* (1931); *Death and Taxes and Other Poems* in *Not So Deep as a Well* (1936); *The Portable Dorothy Parker* (1944); and from *Bookman, Life, McCall's, Nation, New Republic, The New Yorker, New York Herald Tribune, New York World, Saturday Evening Post, Saturday Review, Vanity Fair, Vogue,* and *Yale Review*. In 1936, Parker added one poem to *Enough Rope* and five to *Death and Taxes*, and renamed the collection *Death and Taxes and Other Poems*. In 1944 she added only one previously uncollected poem to *The Portable Dorothy Parker*, "War Song." The texts and order of the poems in the original collections are retained intact; the additions that appear in *Not So Deep as a Well* are included at the end of each collection. Parker continued to write for magazines until her death in 1967, but there was no complete collection of her work until Penguin's *Complete Stories* in 1995. This volume is the first complete collection of her poems.

COMPLETE POEMS

ENOUGH ROPE

(1926)

THRENODY

Lilacs blossom just as sweet
Now my heart is shattered.
If I bowled it down the street,
Who's to say it mattered?
If there's one that rode away
What would I be missing?
Lips that taste of tears, they say,
Are the best for kissing.

Eyes that watch the morning star
Seem a little brighter;
Arms held out to darkness are
Usually whiter.
Shall I bar the strolling guest,
Bind my brow with willow,
When, they say, the empty breast
Is the softer pillow?

That a heart falls tinkling down,
Never think it ceases.
Every likely lad in town
Gathers up the pieces.
If there's one gone whistling by
Would I let it grieve me?
Let him wonder if I lie;
Let him half believe me.

THE SMALL HOURS

No more my little song comes back;
    And now of nights I lay
My head on down, to watch the black
    And wait the unfailing gray.

Oh, sad are winter nights, and slow;
    And sad's a song that's dumb;
And sad it is to lie and know
    Another dawn will come.

THE FALSE FRIENDS

They laid their hands upon my head,
They stroked my cheek and brow;
And time could heal a hurt, they said,
And time could dim a vow.

And they were pitiful and mild
Who whispered to me then,
"The heart that breaks in April, child,
Will mend in May again."

Oh, many a mended heart they knew,
So old they were, and wise.
And little did they have to do
To come to me with lies!

Who flings me silly talk of May
Shall meet a bitter soul;
For June was nearly spent away
Before my heart was whole.

THE TRIFLER

Death's the lover that I'd be taking;
   Wild and fickle and fierce is he.
Small's his care if my heart be breaking—
   Gay young Death would have none of me.

Hear them clack of my haste to greet him!
   No one other my mouth had kissed.
I had dressed me in silk to meet him—
   False young Death would not hold the tryst.

Slow's the blood that was quick and stormy,
   Smooth and cold is the bridal bed;
I must wait till he whistles for me—
   Proud young Death would not turn his head.

I must wait till my breast is wilted,
   I must wait till my back is bowed,
I must rock in the corner, jilted,—
   Death went galloping down the road.

Gone's my heart with a trifling rover.
   Fine he was in the game he played—
Kissed, and promised, and threw me over,
   And rode away with a prettier maid.

A VERY SHORT SONG

Once, when I was young and true,
   Someone left me sad—
Broke my brittle heart in two;
   And that is very bad.

Love is for unlucky folk,
   Love is but a curse.
Once there was a heart I broke;
   And that, I think, is worse.

A WELL-WORN STORY

In April, in April,
My one love came along,
And I ran the slope of my high hill
To follow a thread of song.

His eyes were hard as porphyry
With looking on cruel lands;
His voice went slipping over me
Like terrible silver hands.

Together we trod the secret lane
And walked the muttering town.
I wore my heart like a wet, red stain
On the breast of a velvet gown.

In April, in April,
My love went whistling by,
And I stumbled here to my high hill
Along the way of a lie.

Now what should I do in this place
But sit and count the chimes,
And splash cold water on my face
And spoil a page with rhymes?

CONVALESCENT

How shall I wail, that wasn't meant for weeping?
Love has run and left me, oh, what then?
Dream, then, I must, who never can be sleeping;
What if I should meet Love, once again?

What if I met him, walking on the highway?
Let him see how lightly I should care.
He'd travel his way, I would follow my way;
Hum a little song, and pass him there.

What if at night, beneath a sky of ashes,
He should seek my doorstep, pale with need?
There could he lie, and dry would be my lashes;
Let him stop his noise, and let me read.

Oh, but I'm gay, that's better off without him;
Would he'd come and see me, laughing here.
Lord! Don't I know I'd have my arms about him,
Crying to him, "Oh, come in, my dear!"

THE DARK GIRL'S RHYME

Who was there had seen us
   Wouldn't bid him run?
Heavy lay between us
   All our sires had done.

There he was, a-springing
   Of a pious race—
Setting hags a-swinging
   In a market-place;

Sowing turnips over
   Where the poppies lay;
Looking past the clover,
   Adding up the hay;

Shouting through the Spring song,
   Clumping down the sod;
Toadying, in sing-song,
   To a crabbèd god.

There I was, that came of
   Folk of mud and flame—
I that had my name of
   Them without a name.

Up and down a mountain
   Streeled my silly stock;
Passing by a fountain,
   Wringing at a rock;

Devil-gotten sinners,
    Throwing back their heads;
Fiddling for their dinners,
    Kissing for their beds.

Not a one had seen us
    Wouldn't help him flee.
Angry ran between us
    Blood of him and me.

How shall I be mating
    Who have looked above—
Living for a hating,
    Dying of a love?

EPITAPH

The first time I died, I walked my ways;
I followed the file of limping days.

I held me tall, with my head flung up,
But I dared not look on the new moon's cup.

I dared not look on the sweet young rain,
And between my ribs was a gleaming pain.

The next time I died, they laid me deep.
They spoke worn words to hallow my sleep.

They tossed me petals, they wreathed me fern,
They weighted me down with a marble urn.

And I lie here warm, and I lie here dry,
And watch the worms slip by, slip by.

LIGHT OF LOVE

Joy stayed with me a night—
Young and free and fair—
And in the morning light
He left me there.

Then Sorrow came to stay,
And lay upon my breast;
He walked with me in the day,
And knew me best.

I'll never be a bride,
Nor yet celibate,
So I'm living now with Pride—
A cold bedmate.

He must not hear nor see,
Nor could he forgive
That Sorrow still visits me
Each day I live.

WAIL

Love has gone a-rocketing.
   That is not the worst;
I could do without the thing,
   And not be the first.

Joy has gone the way it came.
   That is nothing new;
I could get along the same,—
   Many people do.

Dig for me the narrow bed,
   Now I am bereft.
All my pretty hates are dead,
   And what have I left?

THE SATIN DRESS

Needle, needle, dip and dart,
Thrusting up and down,
Where's the man could ease a heart
Like a satin gown?

See the stitches curve and crawl
Round the cunning seams—
Patterns thin and sweet and small
As a lady's dreams.

Wantons go in bright brocades;
Brides in organdie;
Gingham's for the plighted maid;
Satin's for the free!

Wool's to line a miser's chest;
Crape's to calm the old;
Velvet hides an empty breast;
Satin's for the bold!

Lawn is for a bishop's yoke;
Linen's for a nun;
Satin is for wiser folk—
Would the dress were done!

Satin glows in candle-light—
Satin's for the proud!
They will say who watch at night,
"What a fine shroud!"

SOMEBODY'S SONG

This is what I vow:
He shall have my heart to keep;
Sweetly will we stir and sleep,
    All the years, as now.
Swift the measured sands may run;
Love like this is never done;
He and I are welded one:
    This is what I vow.

This is what I pray:
Keep him by me tenderly;
Keep him sweet in pride of me,
    Ever and a day;
Keep me from the old distress;
Let me, for our happiness,
Be the one to love the less:
    This is what I pray.

This is what I know:
Lovers' oaths are thin as rain;
Love's a harbinger of pain—
    Would it were not so!
Ever is my heart a-thirst,
Ever is my love accurst;
He is neither last nor first—
    This is what I know.

ANECDOTE

So silent I when Love was by
    He yawned, and turned away;
But Sorrow clings to my apron-strings,
    I have so much to say.

BRAGGART

The days will rally, wreathing
Their crazy tarantelle;
And you must go on breathing,
But I'll be safe in hell.

Like January weather,
The years will bite and smart,
And pull your bones together
To wrap your chattering heart.

The pretty stuff you're made of
Will crack and crease and dry.
The thing you are afraid of
Will look from every eye.

You will go faltering after
The bright, imperious line,
And split your throat on laughter,
And burn your eyes with brine.

You will be frail and musty
With peering, furtive head,
Whilst I am young and lusty
Among the roaring dead.

EPITAPH FOR A DARLING LADY

All her hours were yellow sands,
Blown in foolish whorls and tassels;
Slipping warmly through her hands;
Patted into little castles.

Shiny day on shiny day
Tumble in a rainbow clutter,
As she flipped them all away,
Sent them spinning down the gutter.

Leave for her a red young rose,
Go your way, and save your pity;
She is happy, for she knows
That her dust is very pretty.

TO A MUCH TOO UNFORTUNATE LADY

He will love you presently
If you be the way you be.
Send your heart a-skittering,
He will stoop, and lift the thing.
Be your dreams as thread, to tease
Into patterns he shall please.
Let him see your passion is
Ever tenderer than his. . . .
Go and bless your star above,
Thus are you, and thus is Love.

He will leave you white with woe,
If you go the way you go.
If your dreams were thread to weave,
He will pluck them from his sleeve.
If your heart had come to rest,
He will flick it from his breast.
Tender though the love he bore,
You had loved a little more. . . .
Lady, go and curse your star,
Thus Love is, and thus you are.

PATHS

I shall tread, another year,
   Ways I walked with Grief,
Past the dry, ungarnered ear
   And the brittle leaf.

I shall stand, a year apart,
   Wondering, and shy,
Thinking, "Here she broke her heart;
   Here she pled to die."

I shall hear the pheasants call,
   And the raucous geese;
Down these ways, another Fall,
   I shall walk with Peace.

But the pretty path I trod
   Hand-in-hand with Love,—
Underfoot, the nascent sod,
   Brave young boughs above,

And the stripes of ribbon grass
   By the curling way,—
I shall never dare to pass
   To my dying day.

HEARTHSIDE

Half across the world from me
Lie the lands I'll never see—
I, whose longing lives and dies
Where a ship has sailed away;
I, that never close my eyes
But to look upon Cathay.

Things I may not know nor tell
Wait, where older waters swell;
Ways that flowered at Sappho's tread,
Winds that sighed in Homer's strings,
Vibrant with the singing dead,
Golden with the dust of wings.

Under deeper skies than mine,
Quiet valleys dip and shine.
Where their tender grasses heal
Ancient scars of trench and tomb
I shall never walk; nor kneel
Where the bones of poets bloom.

If I seek a lovelier part,
Where I travel goes my heart;
Where I stray my thought must go;
With me wanders my desire.
Best to sit and watch the snow,
Turn the lock, and poke the fire.

THE NEW LOVE

If it shine or if it rain,
  Little will I care or know.
Days, like drops upon a pane,
  Slip, and join, and go.

At my door's another lad;
  Here's his flower in my hair.
If he see me pale and sad,
  Will he see me fair?

I sit looking at the floor.
  Little will I think or say
If he seek another door;
  Even if he stay.

RAINY NIGHT

Ghosts of all my lovely sins,
  Who attend too well my pillow,
Gay the wanton rain begins;
  Hide the limp and tearful willow,

Turn aside your eyes and ears,
  Trail away your robes of sorrow.
You shall have my further years,—
  You shall walk with me to-morrow.

I am sister to the rain;
  Fey and sudden and unholy,
Petulant at the windowpane,
  Quickly lost, remembered slowly.

I have lived with shades, a shade;
  I am hung with graveyard flowers.
Let me be to-night arrayed
  In the silver of the showers.

Every fragile thing shall rust;
  When another April passes
I may be a furry dust,
  Sifting through the brittle grasses.

All sweet sins shall be forgot
  Who will live to tell their siring?
Hear me now, nor let me rot
  Wistful still, and still aspiring.

Ghosts of dear temptations, heed;
   I am frail, be you forgiving.
See you not that I have need
   To be living with the living?

Sail, to-night, the Styx's breast;
   Glide among the dim processions
Of the exquisite unblest.
   Spirits of my shared transgressions.

Roam with young Persephone,
   Plucking poppies for your slumber . . .
With the morrow, there shall be
   One more wraith among your number.

FOR A SAD LADY

And let her loves, when she is dead,
Write this above her bones:
"No more she lives to give us bread
Who asked her only stones."

RECURRENCE

We shall have our little day.
Take my hand and travel still
Round and round the little way,
Up and down the little hill.

It is good to love again;
Scan the renovated skies,
Dip and drive the idling pen,
Sweetly tint the paling lies.

Trace the dripping, piercèd heart,
Speak the fair, insistent verse,
Vow to God, and slip apart,
Little better, little worse.

Would we need not know before
How shall end this prettiness;
One of us must love the more,
One of us shall love the less.

Thus it is, and so it goes;
We shall have our day, my dear.
Where, unwilling, dies the rose
Buds the new, another year.

STORY OF MRS. W———

My garden blossoms pink and white,
   A place of decorous murmuring
Where I am safe from August night
   And cannot feel the knife of spring.

And I may walk the pretty place
   Before the curtsying hollyhocks
And laundered daisies, round of face—
   Good little girls, in party frocks.

My trees are amiably arrayed
   In pattern on the dappled sky,
And I may sit in filtered shade
   And watch the tidy years go by.

And I may amble pleasantly
   And hear my neighbors list their bones
And click my tongue in sympathy,
   And count the cracks in paving stones.

My door is grave in oaken strength,
   The cool of linen calms my bed,
And there at night I stretch my length
   And envy no one but the dead.

THE DRAMATISTS

A string of shiny days we had,
   A spotless sky, a yellow sun;
And neither you nor I was sad
   When that was through and done.

But when, one day, a boy comes by
   And pleads me with your happiest vow,
"There was a lad I knew—" I'll sigh;
   "I do not know him now."

And when another girl shall pass
   And speak a little name I said,
Then you will say "There was a lass—
   I wonder is she dead."

And each of us will sigh, and start
   A-talking of a faded year,
And lay a hand above a heart,
   And dry a pretty tear.

AUGUST

When my eyes are weeds,
And my lips are petals, spinning
Down the wind that has beginning
Where the crumpled beeches start
In a fringe of salty reeds;
When my arms are elder-bushes,
And the rangy lilac pushes
Upward, upward through my heart;

Summer, do your worst!
Light your tinsel moon, and call on
Your performing stars to fall on
Headlong through your paper sky;
Nevermore shall I be cursed
By a flushed and amorous slattern,
With her dusty laces' pattern
Trailing, as she straggles by.

THE WHITE LADY

I cannot rest, I cannot rest
   In strait and shiny wood,
My woven hands upon my breast—
   The dead are all so good!

The earth is cool across their eyes;
   They lie there quietly.
But I am neither old nor wise,
   They do not welcome me.

Where never I walked alone before
   I wander in the weeds;
And people scream and bar the door,
   And rattle at their beads.

We cannot rest, we never rest
   Within a narrow bed
Who still must love the living best—
   Who hate the drowsy dead!

I KNOW I HAVE BEEN HAPPIEST

I know I have been happiest at your side;
But what is done, is done, and all's to be.
And small the good, to linger dolefully,—
Gaily it lived, and gallantly it died.
I will not make you songs of hearts denied,
And you, being man, would have no tears of me,
And should I offer you fidelity,
You'd be, I think, a little terrified.

Yet this the need of woman, this her curse:
To range her little gifts, and give, and give,
Because the throb of giving's sweet to bear.
To you, who never begged me vows or verse,
My gift shall be my absence, while I live;
But after that, my dear, I cannot swear.

TESTAMENT

Oh, let it be a night of lyric rain
And singing breezes, when my bell is tolled.
I have so loved the rain that I would hold
Last in my ears its friendly, dim refrain.
I shall lie cool and quiet, who have lain
Fevered, and watched the book of day unfold.
Death will not see me flinch; the heart is bold
That pain has made incapable of pain.

Kinder the busy worms than ever love;
It will be peace to lie there, empty-eyed,
My bed made secret by the leveling showers,
My breast replenishing the weeds above.
And you will say of me, "Then has she died?
Perhaps I should have sent a spray of flowers."

"I SHALL COME BACK"

I shall come back without fanfaronade
Of wailing wind and graveyard panoply;
But, trembling, slip from cool Eternity—
A mild and most bewildered little shade.
I shall not make sepulchral midnight raid,
But softly come where I had longed to be
In April twilight's unsung melody,
And I, not you, shall be the one afraid.

Strange, that from lovely dreamings of the dead
I shall come back to you, who hurt me most.
You may not feel my hand upon your head,
I'll be so new and inexpert a ghost.
Perhaps you will not know that I am near,—
And that will break my ghostly heart, my dear.

CONDOLENCE

They hurried here, as soon as you had died,
Their faces damp with haste and sympathy,
And pressed my hand in theirs, and smoothed my knee,
And clicked their tongues, and watched me, mournful-eyed.
Gently they told me of that Other Side—
How, even then, you waited there for me,
And what ecstatic meeting ours would be.
Moved by the lovely tale, they broke, and cried.

And when I smiled, they told me I was brave,
And they rejoiced that I was comforted,
And left, to tell of all the help they gave.
But I had smiled to think how you, the dead,
So curiously preoccupied and grave,
Would laugh, could you have heard the things they said.

THE IMMORTALS

If you should sail for Trebizond, or die,
Or cry another name in your first sleep,
Or see me board a train, and fail to sigh,
Appropriately, I'd clutch my breast and weep
And you, if I should wander through the door,
Or sin, or seek a nunnery, or save
My lips and give my cheek, would tread the floor
And aptly mention poison and the grave.

Therefore the mooning world is gratified,
Quoting how prettily we sigh and swear;
And you and I, correctly side by side,
Shall live as lovers when our bones are bare;
And though we lie forever enemies,
Shall rank with Abélard and Héloïse.

A PORTRAIT

Because my love is quick to come and go—
A little here, and then a little there—
What use are any words of mine to swear
My heart is stubborn, and my spirit slow
Of weathering the drip and drive of woe?
What is my oath, when you have but to bare
My little, easy loves; and I can dare
Only to shrug, and answer, "They are so"?

You do not know how heavy a heart it is
That hangs about my neck—a clumsy stone
Cut with a birth, a death, a bridal-day.
Each time I love, I find it still my own,
Who take it, now to that lad, now to this,
Seeking to give the wretched thing away.

PORTRAIT OF THE ARTIST

Oh, lead me to a quiet cell
   Where never footfall rankles,
And bar the window passing well,
   And gyve my wrists and ankles.

Oh, wrap my eyes with linen fair,
   With hempen cord go bind me,
And, of your mercy, leave me there,
   Nor tell them where to find me.

Oh, lock the portal as you go,
   And see its bolts be double. . . .
Come back in half an hour or so,
   And I will be in trouble.

CHANT FOR DARK HOURS

Some men, some men
Cannot pass a
Book shop.
(Lady, make your mind up, and wait your life away.)

Some men, some men
Cannot pass a
Crap game.
(He said he'd come at moonrise, and here's another day!)

Some men, some men
Cannot pass a
Bar-room.
(Wait about, and hang about, and that's the way it goes.)

Some men, some men
Cannot pass a
Woman.
(Heaven never send me another one of those!)

Some men, some men
Cannot pass a
Golf course.
(Read a book, and sew a seam, and slumber if you can.)

Some men, some men
Cannot pass a
Haberdasher's.
(All your life you wait around for some damn man!)

UNFORTUNATE COINCIDENCE

By the time you swear you're his,
   Shivering and sighing,
And he vows his passion is
   Infinite, undying—
Lady, make a note of this:
   One of you is lying.

VERSE REPORTING LATE ARRIVAL
AT A CONCLUSION

Consider a lady gone reckless in love,
    In novels and plays:
You watch her proceed in a drapery of
    A roseate haze.
Acclaimed as a riot, a wow, and a scream,
She flies with her beau to les Alpes Maritimes,
And moves in a mist of a mutual dream
    The rest of her days.

In life, if you'll listen to one who has been
    Observant of such,
A lady in love is more frequently in
    Decidedly Dutch.
The thorn, so to say, is revealed by the rose.
The best that she gets is a sock in the nose.
These authors and playwrights, I'm forced to suppose,
    Don't get around much.

INVENTORY

Four be the things I am wiser to know:
Idleness, sorrow, a friend, and a foe.

Four be the things I'd been better without:
Love, curiosity, freckles, and doubt.

Three be the things I shall never attain:
Envy, content, and sufficient champagne.

Three be the things I shall have till I die:
Laughter and hope and a sock in the eye.

NOW AT LIBERTY

Little white love, your way you've taken;
   Now I am left alone, alone.
Little white love, my heart's forsaken.
   (Whom shall I get by telephone?)
Well do I know there's no returning;
   Once you go out, it's done, it's done.
All of my days are gray with yearning.
   (Nevertheless, a girl needs fun.)

Little white love, perplexed and weary,
   Sadly your banner fluttered down.
Sullen the days, and dreary, dreary.
   (Which of the boys is still in town?)
Radiant and sure, you came a-flying;
   Puzzled, you left on lagging feet.
Slow in my breast, my heart is dying.
   (Nevertheless, a girl must eat.)

Little white love, I hailed you gladly;
   Now I must wave you out of sight.
Ah, but you used me badly, badly.
   (Who'd like to take me out to-night?)
All of the blundering words I've spoken,
   Little white love, forgive, forgive.
Once you went out, my heart fell, broken.
   (Nevertheless, a girl must live.)

COMMENT

Oh, life is a glorious cycle of song,
A medley of extemporanea;
And love is a thing that can never go wrong;
And I am Marie of Roumania.

PLEA

Secrets, you said, would hold us two apart;
   You'd have me know of you your least transgression
And so the intimate places of your heart,
   Kneeling, you bared to me, as in confession.
Softly you told of loves that went before,—
   Of clinging arms, of kisses gladly given;
Luxuriously clean of heart once more,
   You rose up, then, and stood before me, shriven.

When this, my day of happiness, is through,
   And love, that bloomed so fair, turns brown and brittle,
There is a thing that I shall ask of you—
   I, who have given so much, and asked so little.
Some day, when there's another in my stead;
   Again you'll feel the need of absolution,
And you will go to her, and bow your head,
   And offer her your past, as contribution.

When with your list of loves you overcome her,
For Heaven's sake, keep this one secret from her!

PATTERN

Leave me to my lonely pillow.
   Go, and take your silly posies;
Who has vowed to wear the willow
   Looks a fool, tricked out in roses.

Who are you, my lad, to ease me?
   Leave your pretty words unspoken.
Tinkling echoes little please me,
   Now my heart is freshly broken.

Over young are you to guide me,
   And your blood is slow and sleeping.
If you must, then sit beside me. . . .
   Tell me, why have I been weeping?

DE PROFUNDIS

Oh, is it, then, Utopian
To hope that I may meet a man
Who'll not relate, in accents suave,
The tales of girls he used to have?

THEY PART

And if, my friend, you'd have it end,
    There's naught to hear or tell.
But need you try to black my eye
    In wishing me farewell?

Though I admit an edgèd wit
    In woe is warranted,
May I be frank? . . . Such words as "———"
    Are better left unsaid.

There's rosemary for you and me;
    But is it usual, dear,
To hire a man, and fill a van
    By way of *souvenir?*

BALLADE OF A GREAT WEARINESS

There's little to have but the things I had,
　　There's little to bear but the things I bore.
There's nothing to carry and naught to add,
　　And glory to Heaven, I paid the score.
There's little to do but I did before,
　　There's little to learn but the things I know;
And this is the sum of a lasting lore:
　　Scratch a lover, and find a foe.

And couldn't it be I was young and mad
　　If ever my heart on my sleeve I wore?
There's many to claw at a heart unclad,
　　And little the wonder it ripped and tore.
There's one that'll join in their push and roar,
　　With stories to jabber, and stones to throw;
He'll fetch you a lesson that costs you sore—
　　Scratch a lover, and find a foe.

So little I'll offer to you, my lad;
　　It's little in loving I set my store.
There's many a maid would be flushed and glad,
　　And better you'll knock at a kindlier door.
I'll dig at my lettuce, and sweep my floor—
　　Forever, forever I'm done with woe—
And happen I'll whistle about my chore,
　　"Scratch a lover and find a foe."

L'Envoi:
Oh, beggar or prince, no more, no more!
    Be off and away with your strut and show.
The sweeter the apple, the blacker the core—
    Scratch a lover, and find a foe!

RÉSUMÉ

Razors pain you;
Rivers are damp;
Acids stain you;
And drugs cause cramp.
Guns aren't lawful;
Nooses give;
Gas smells awful;
You might as well live.

RENUNCIATION

Chloe's hair, no doubt, was brighter;
   Lydia's mouth more sweetly sad;
Hebe's arms were rather whiter;
   Languorous-lidded Helen had
Eyes more blue than e'er the sky was;
Lalage's was subtler stuff;
Still, you used to think that I was
   Fair enough.

Now you're casting yearning glances
   At the pale Penelope;
Cutting in on Claudia's dances;
   Taking Iris out to tea.
Iole you find warm-hearted;
   Zoë's cheek is far from rough,—
Don't you think it's time we parted? . . .
   Fair enough!

DAY-DREAMS

We'd build a little bungalow,
If you and I were one,
And carefully we'd plan it, so
We'd get the morning sun.
I'd rise each day at rosy dawn
And bustle gaily down;
In evening's cool, you'd spray the lawn
When you came back from town.

A little cook-book I should buy,
Your dishes I'd prepare;
And though they came out black and dry,
I know you wouldn't care.
How valiantly I'd strive to learn,
Assured you'd not complain!
And if my finger I should burn,
You'd kiss away the pain.

I'd buy a little scrubbing-brush
And beautify the floors;
I'd warble gaily as a thrush
About my little chores.
But though I'd cook and sew and scrub,
A higher life I'd find;
I'd join a little women's club
And cultivate my mind.

If you and I were one, my dear,
A model life we'd lead.
We'd travel on, from year to year,
At no increase of speed.
Ah, clear to me the vision of
The things that we should do!
And so I think it best, my love,
To string along as two.

THE VETERAN

When I was young and bold and strong,
Oh, right was right, and wrong was wrong!
My plume on high, my flag unfurled,
I rode away to right the world.
"Come out, you dogs, and fight!" said I,
And wept there was but once to die.

But I am old; and good and bad
Are woven in a crazy plaid.
I sit and say, "The world is so;
And he is wise who lets it go.
A battle lost, a battle won—
The difference is small, my son."

Inertia rides and riddles me;
The which is called Philosophy.

PROPHETIC SOUL

Because your eyes are slant and slow
    Because your hair is sweet to touch,
My heart is high again; but oh,
    I doubt if this will get me much.

VERSE FOR A CERTAIN DOG

Such glorious faith as fills your limpid eyes,
　　Dear little friend of mine, I never knew.
All-innocent are you, and yet all-wise.
　　(For heaven's sake, stop worrying that shoe!)
You look about, and all you see is fair;
　　This mighty globe was made for you alone.
Of all the thunderous ages, you're the heir.
　　(Get off the pillow with that dirty bone!)

A skeptic world you face with steady gaze;
　　High in young pride you hold your noble head;
Gayly you meet the rush of roaring days.
　　(*Must* you eat puppy biscuit on the bed?)
Lancelike your courage, gleaming swift and strong,
　　Yours the white rapture of a wingèd soul,
Yours is a spirit like a May-day song.
　　(God help you, if you break the goldfish bowl!)

"Whatever is, is good," your gracious creed.
　　You wear your joy of living like a crown.
Love lights your simplest act, your every deed.
　　(Drop it, I tell you—put that kitten down!)
You are God's kindliest gift of all,—a friend.
　　Your shining loyalty unflecked by doubt,
You ask but leave to follow to the end.
　　(Couldn't you wait until I took you out?)

FOLK TUNE

Other lads, their ways are daring:
   Other lads, they're not afraid;
Other lads, they show they're caring;
   Other lads—they know a maid.
Wiser Jock than ever you were,
   Will's with gayer spirit blest,
Robin's kindlier and truer,—
   Why should I love you the best?

Other lads, their eyes are bolder.
   Young they are, and strong and slim,
Ned is straight and broad of shoulder,
   Donald has a way with him.
David stands a head above you,
   Dick's as brave as Lancelot,—
Why, ah why, then, should I love you?
   Naturally, I do not.

GODSPEED

Oh, seek, my love, your newer way;
   I'll not be left in sorrow.
So long as I have yesterday,
   Go take your damned to-morrow!

SONG OF PERFECT PROPRIETY

Oh, I should like to ride the seas,
   A roaring buccaneer;
A cutlass banging at my knees,
   A dirk behind my ear.
And when my captives' chains would clank
   I'd howl with glee and drink,
And then fling out the quivering plank
   And watch the beggars sink.

I'd like to straddle gory decks,
   And dig in laden sands,
And know the feel of throbbing necks
   Between my knotted hands.
Oh, I should like to strut and curse
   Among my blackguard crew. . . .
But I am writing little verse,
   As little ladies do.

Oh, I should like to dance and laugh
   And pose and preen and sway,
And rip the hearts of men in half,
   And toss the bits away.
I'd like to view the reeling years
   Through unastonished eyes,
And dip my finger-tips in tears,
   And give my smiles for sighs.

I'd stroll beyond the ancient bounds,
   And tap at fastened gates,
And hear the prettiest of sounds,—
   The clink of shattered fates.
My slaves I'd like to bind with thongs
   That cut and burn and chill. . . .
But I am writing little songs,
   As little ladies will.

SOCIAL NOTE

Lady, lady, should you meet
One whose ways are all discreet,
One who murmurs that his wife
Is the lodestar of his life,
One who keeps assuring you
That he never was untrue,
Never loved another one . . .
Lady, lady, better run!

ONE PERFECT ROSE

A single flow'r he sent me, since we met.
  All tenderly his messenger he chose;
Deep-hearted, pure, with scented dew still wet—
  One perfect rose.

I knew the language of the floweret;
  "My fragile leaves," it said, "his heart enclose."
Love long has taken for his amulet
  One perfect rose.

Why is it no one ever sent me yet
  One perfect limousine, do you suppose?
Ah no, it's always just my luck to get
  One perfect rose.

BALLADE AT THIRTY-FIVE

This, no song of an ingénue,
    This, no ballad of innocence;
This, the rhyme of a lady who
    Followed ever her natural bents.
    This, a solo of sapience,
This, a chantey of sophistry,
    This, the sum of experiments,—
I loved them until they loved me.

Decked in garments of sable hue,
    Daubed with ashes of myriad Lents,
Wearing shower bouquets of rue,
    Walk I ever in penitence.
    Oft I roam, as my heart repents,
Through God's acre of memory,
    Marking stones, in my reverence,
"I loved them until they loved me."

Pictures pass me in long review,—
    Marching columns of dead events.
I was tender, and, often, true;
    Ever a prey to coincidence.
    Always knew I the consequence;
Always saw what the end would be.
    We're as Nature has made us—hence
I loved them until they loved me.

L'Envoi:
Princes, never I'd give offense,
   Won't you think of me tenderly?
Here's my strength and my weakness, gents,—
   I loved them until they loved me.

THE THIN EDGE

With you, my heart is quiet here,
And all my thoughts are cool as rain.
I sit and let the shifting year
Go by before the window-pane,
And reach my hand to yours, my dear . . .
I wonder what it's like in Spain.

SPRING SONG

(IN THE EXPECTED MANNER)

Enter April, laughingly,
　　Blossoms in her tumbled hair,
High of heart, and fancy-free—
　　When was maiden half so fair?
Bright her eyes with easy tears,
　　Wanton-sweet, her smiles for men.
"Winter's gone," she cries, "and here's
　　Spring again."

When we loved, 'twas April, too;
　　Madcap April—urged us on.
Just as she did, so did you—
　　Sighed, and smiled, and then were gone.
How she plied her pretty arts,
　　How she laughed and sparkled then!
April, make love in our hearts
　　Spring again!

LOVE SONG

My own dear love, he is strong and bold
    And he cares not what comes after.
His words ring sweet as a chime of gold,
    And his eyes are lit with laughter.
He is jubilant as a flag unfurled—
    Oh, a girl, she'd not forget him.
My own dear love, he is all my world,—
    And I wish I'd never met him.

My love, he's mad, and my love, he's fleet,
    And a wild young wood-thing bore him!
The ways are fair to his roaming feet,
    And the skies are sunlit for him.
As sharply sweet to my heart he seems
    As the fragrance of acacia.
My own dear love, he is all my dreams,—
    And I wish he were in Asia.

My love runs by like a day in June,
    And he makes no friends of sorrows.
He'll tread his galloping rigadoon
    In the pathway of the morrows.
He'll live his days where the sunbeams start,
    Nor could storm or wind uproot him.
My own dear love, he is all my heart,—
    And I wish somebody'd shoot him.

INDIAN SUMMER

In youth, it was a way I had
     To do my best to please,
And change, with every passing lad,
     To suit his theories.

But now I know the things I know,
     And do the things I do;
And if you do not like me so,
     To hell, my love, with you!

PHILOSOPHY

If I should labor through daylight and dark,
     Consecrate, valorous, serious, true,
Then on the world I may blazon my mark;
     And what if I don't, and what if I do?

FOR AN UNKNOWN LADY

Lady, if you'd slumber sound,
Keep your eyes upon the ground.
If you'd toss and turn at night,
Slip your glances left and right.
Would the mornings find you gay,
Never give your heart away.
Would they find you pale and sad,
Fling it to a whistling lad.
Ah, but when his pleadings burn,
Will you let my words return?
Will you lock your pretty lips,
And deny your finger-tips,
Veil away your tender eyes,
Just because some words were wise?
If he whistles low and clear
When the insistent moon is near
And the secret stars are known,—
Will your heart be still your own
Just because some words were true? . . .
Lady, I was told them, too!

THE LEAL

The friends I made have slipped and strayed,
   And who's the one that cares?
A trifling lot and best forgot—
   And that's my tale, and theirs.

Then if my friendships break and bend,
   There's little need to cry
The while I know that every foe
   Is faithful till I die.

FINIS

Now it's over, and now it's done;
  Why does everything look the same?
Just as bright, the unheeding sun,—
  Can't it see that the parting came?
People hurry and work and swear,
  Laugh and grumble and die and wed,
Ponder what they will eat and wear,—
  Don't they know that our love is dead?

Just as busy, the crowded street;
  Cars and wagons go rolling on,
Children chuckle, and lovers meet,—
  Don't they know that our love is gone?
No one pauses to pay a tear;
  None walks slow, for the love that's through,—
I might mention, my recent dear,
  I've reverted to normal, too.

WORDS OF COMFORT TO BE
SCRATCHED ON A MIRROR

Helen of Troy had a wandering glance;
Sappho's restriction was only the sky;
Ninon was ever the chatter of France;
But oh, what a good girl am I!

MEN

They hail you as their morning star
Because you are the way you are.
If you return the sentiment,
They'll try to make you different;
And once they have you, safe and sound,
They want to change you all around.
Your moods and ways they put a curse on;
They'd make of you another person.
They cannot let you go your gait;
They influence and educate.
They'd alter all that they admired.
They make me sick, they make me tired.

NEWS ITEM

Men seldom make passes
At girls who wear glasses.

SONG OF ONE OF THE GIRLS

Here in my heart I am Helen;
  I'm Aspasia and Hero, at least.
I'm Judith, and Jael, and Madame de Staël;
  I'm Salomé, moon of the East.

Here in my soul I am Sappho;
  Lady Hamilton am I, as well.
In me Récamier vies with Kitty O'Shea,
  With Dido, and Eve, and poor Nell.

I'm of the glamorous ladies
  At whose beckoning history shook.
But you are a man, and see only my pan,
  So I stay at home with a book.

LULLABY

Sleep, pretty lady, the night is enfolding you,
    Drift, and so lightly, on crystalline streams.
Wrapped in its perfumes, the darkness is holding you;
    Starlight bespangles the way of your dreams.
Chorus the nightingales, wistfully amorous;
    Blessedly quiet, the blare of the day.
All the sweet hours may your visions be glamorous,—
    Sleep, pretty lady, as long as you may.

Sleep, pretty lady, the night shall be still for you;
    Silvered and silent, it watches your rest.
Each little breeze, in its eagerness, will for you
    Murmur the melodies ancient and blest.
So in the midnight does happiness capture us;
    Morning is dim with another day's tears.
Give yourself sweetly to images rapturous,—
    Sleep, pretty lady, a couple of years.

Sleep, pretty lady, the world awaits day with you;
    Girlish and golden, the slender young moon.
Grant the fond darkness its mystical way with you,
    Morning returns to us ever too soon.
Roses unfold, in their loveliness, all for you;
    Blossom the lilies for hope of your glance.
When you're awake, all the men go and fall for you,—
    Sleep, pretty lady, and give me a chance.

FAUT DE MIEUX

Travel, trouble, music, art,
    A kiss, a frock, a rhyme,—
I never said they feed my heart,
    But still they pass my time.

ROUNDEL

She's passing fair; but so demure is she
    So quiet is her gown, so smooth her hair,
That few there are who note her and agree
    She's passing fair.

Yet when was ever beauty held more rare
Than simple heart and maiden modesty?
What fostered charms with virtue could compare?

Alas, no lover ever stops to see;
The best that she is offered is the air.
Yet—if the passing mark is minus
        D—
    She's passing fair.

A CERTAIN LADY

Oh, I can smile for you, and tilt my head,
   And drink your rushing words with eager lips,
And paint my mouth for you a fragrant red,
   And trace your brows with tutored finger-tips.
When you rehearse your list of loves to me,
   Oh, I can laugh and marvel, rapturous-eyed.
And you laugh back, nor can you ever see
   The thousand little deaths my heart has died.
And you believe, so well I know my part,
   That I am gay as morning, light as snow,
And all the straining things within my heart
   You'll never know.

Oh, I can laugh and listen, when we meet,
   And you bring tales of fresh adventurings,—
Of ladies delicately indiscreet,
   Of lingering hands, and gently whispered things.
And you are pleased with me, and strive anew
   To sing me sagas of your late delights.
Thus do you want me—marveling, gay, and true,
   Nor do you see my staring eyes of nights.
And when, in search of novelty, you stray,
   Oh, I can kiss you blithely as you go. . . .
And what goes on, my love, while you're away,
   You'll never know.

OBSERVATION

If I don't drive around the park,
I'm pretty sure to make my mark.
If I'm in bed each night by ten,
I may get back my looks again,
If I abstain from fun and such,
I'll probably amount to much,
But I shall stay the way I am,
Because I do not give a damn.

SYMPTOM RECITAL

I do not like my state of mind;
I'm bitter, querulous, unkind.
I hate my legs, I hate my hands,
I do not yearn for lovelier lands.
I dread the dawn's recurrent light;
I hate to go to bed at night.
I snoot at simple, earnest folk.
I cannot take the gentlest joke.
I find no peace in paint or type.
My world is but a lot of tripe.
I'm disillusioned, empty-breasted.
For what I think, I'd be arrested.
I am not sick, I am not well.
My quondam dreams are shot to hell.
My soul is crushed, my spirit sore;
I do not like me any more.
I cavil, quarrel, grumble, grouse.
I ponder on the narrow house.
I shudder at the thought of men. . . .
I'm due to fall in love again.

RONDEAU REDOUBLÉ
(AND SCARCELY WORTH THE TROUBLE, AT THAT)

The same to me are sombre days and gay.
   Though joyous dawns the rosy morn, and bright,
Because my dearest love is gone away
   Within my heart is melancholy night.

My heart beats low in loneliness, despite
   That riotous Summer holds the earth in sway.
In cerements my spirit is bedight;
   The same to me are sombre days and gay.

Though breezes in the rippling grasses play,
   And waves dash high and far in glorious might,
I thrill no longer to the sparkling day,
   Though joyous dawns the rosy morn, and bright.

Ungraceful seems to me the swallow's flight;
   As well might Heaven's blue be sullen gray;
My soul discerns no beauty in their sight
   Because my dearest love is gone away.

Let roses fling afar their crimson spray,
   And virgin daisies splash the fields with white,
Let bloom the poppy hotly as it may,
   Within my heart is melancholy night.

And this, oh love, my pitiable plight
   Whenever from my circling arms you stray;
This little world of mine has lost its light. . . .
   I hope to God, my dear, that you can say
                    The same to me.

AUTOBIOGRAPHY

Oh, both my shoes are shiny new,
   And pristine is my hat;
My dress is 1922. . . .
   My life is all like that.

THE CHOICE

He'd have given me rolling lands,
   Houses of marble, and billowing farms,
Pearls, to trickle between my hands,
   Smoldering rubies, to circle my arms.
You—you'd only a lilting song,
   Only a melody, happy and high,
You were sudden and swift and strong,—
   Never a thought for another had I.

He'd have given me laces rare,
   Dresses that glimmered with frosty sheen,
Shining ribbons to wrap my hair,
   Horses to draw me, as fine as a queen.
You—you'd only to whistle low,
   Gaily I followed wherever you led.
I took you, and I let him go,—
   Somebody ought to examine my head!

BALLADE OF BIG PLANS

She loved him. He knew it.
And love was a game that two could play at.
— "Julia Cane," p. 280.

Once the orioles sang in chorus,
Once the skies were a cloudless blue.
Spring bore blossoms expressly for us,
Stars lined up to spell "Y-O-U."
All the world wore a golden hue,
Life was a thing to be bold and gay at;
Love was the only game I knew,
And love is a game that two can play at.

Now the heavens are scowling o'er us,
Now the blossoms are pale and few.
Love was a rose with thorns that tore us,
Love was a ship without a crew.
Love is untender, and love is untrue,
Love is a moon for a dog to bay at,
Love is the Lady-That's-Known-as-Lou,
And love is a game that two can play at.

Recollections can only bore us;
Now it's over, and now it's through.
Our day is dead as a dinosaurus.
Other the paths that you pursue.
What is the girl in the case to do?
What is she going to spend her day at?
Fun demands, at a minimum, two—
And love is a game that two can play at.

L'Envoi:
Prince, I'm packing away the rue.
I'll give them something to shout "Hooray" at.
I've got somebody else in view:
And love is a game that two can play at.

GENERAL REVIEW
OF THE SEX SITUATION

Woman wants monogamy;
Man delights in novelty.
Love is woman's moon and sun;
Man has other forms of fun.
Woman lives but in her lord;
Count to ten, and man is bored.
With this the gist and sum of it,
What earthly good can come of it?

INSCRIPTION FOR THE CEILING
OF A BEDROOM

Daily dawns another day;
I must up, to make my way.
Though I dress and drink and eat,
Move my fingers and my feet,
Learn a little, here and there,
Weep and laugh and sweat and swear,
Hear a song, or watch a stage,
Leave some words upon a page,
Claim a foe, or hail a friend—
Bed awaits me at the end.

Though I go in pride and strength,
I'll come back to bed at length.
Though I walk in blinded woe,
Back to bed I'm bound to go.
High my heart, or bowed my head,
All my days but lead to bed.
Up, and out, and on; and then
Ever back to bed again,
Summer, Winter, Spring, and Fall—
I'm a fool to rise at all!

PICTURES IN THE SMOKE

Oh, gallant was the first love, and glittering and fine;
  The second love was water, in a clear white cup;
The third love was his, and the fourth was mine;
  And after that, I always get them all mixed up.

BIOGRAPHIES

1

Now this is the story of Lucy Brown,
A glittering jewel in virtue's crown.
From earliest youth, she aspired to please.
She never fell down and dirtied her knees;
She put all her pennies in savings banks;
She never omitted her "please" and "thanks";
She swallowed her spinach without a squawk;
And patiently listened to Teacher's talk;
She thoughtfully stepped over worms and ants;
And earnestly watered the potted plants;
She didn't dismember expensive toys;
And never would play with the little boys.

And when to young womanhood Lucy came
Her mode of behavior was just the same.
She always was safe in her home at dark;
And never went riding around the park;
She wouldn't put powder upon her nose;
And petticoats sheltered her spotless hose;
She knew how to market and mend and sweep;
By quarter-past ten, she was sound asleep;
In presence of elders, she held her tongue—
The way that they did when the world was young.
And people remarked, in benign accord,
"You'll see that she gathers her just reward."
Observe, their predictions were more than fair.
She married an affluent millionaire

So gallant and handsome and wise and gay,
And rated in Bradstreet at Double A.
And she lived with him happily all her life,
And made him a perfectly elegant wife.

2

Now Marigold Jones, from her babyhood,
Was bad as the model Miss Brown was good.
She stuck out her tongue at her grieving nurse;
She frequently rifled her Grandma's purse;
She banged on the table and broke the plates;
She jeered at the passing inebriates;
And tore all her dresses and ripped her socks;
And shattered the windows with fair-sized rocks;
The words on the fences she'd memorize;
She blackened her dear little brother's eyes;
And cut off her sister's abundant curls;
And never would play with the little girls.

And when she grew up—as is hardly strange—
Her manner of life underwent no change
But faithfully followed her childhood plan.
And once there was talk of a married man!
She sauntered in public in draperies
Affording no secrecy to her knees;
She constantly uttered what was not true;
She flirted and petted, or what have you;

And, tendered advice by her kind Mamma,
Her answer, I shudder to state, was "Blah!"
And people remarked, in sepulchral tones,
"You'll see what becomes of Marigold Jones."
Observe, their predictions were more than fair.
She married an affluent millionaire
So gallant and handsome and wise and gay,
And rated in Bradstreet at Double A.
And she lived with him happily all her life,
And made him a perfectly elegant wife.

NOCTURNE

Always I knew that it could not last
   (Gathering clouds, and the snowflakes flying),
Now it is part of the golden past;
   (Darkening skies, and the night-wind sighing)
It is but cowardice to pretend.
   Cover with ashes our love's cold crater,—
Always I've known that it had to end
   Sooner or later.

Always I knew it would come like this
   (Pattering rain, and the grasses springing),
Sweeter to you is a new love's kiss
   (Flickering sunshine, and young birds singing).
Gone are the raptures that once we knew,
   Now you are finding a new joy greater,—
Well, I'll be doing the same thing, too,
   Sooner or later.

INTERVIEW

The ladies men admire, I've heard,
Would shudder at a wicked word.
Their candle gives a single light;
They'd rather stay at home at night.
They do not keep awake till three,
Nor read erotic poetry.
They never sanction the impure,
Nor recognize an overture.
They shrink from powders and from paints . . .
So far, I've had no complaints.

SONG IN A MINOR KEY

There's a place I know where the birds swing low,
    And wayward vines go roaming,
Where the lilacs nod, and a marble god
    Is pale, in scented gloaming.
And at sunset there comes a lady fair
    Whose eyes are deep with yearning.
By an old, old gate does the lady wait
    Her own true love's returning.

But the days go by, and the lilacs die,
    And trembling birds seek cover;
Yet the lady stands, with her long white hands
    Held out to greet her lover.
And it's there she'll stay till the shadowy day
    A monument they grave her.
She will always wait by the same old gate,—
    The gate her true love gave her.

EXPERIENCE

Some men break your heart in two,
    Some men fawn and flatter,
Some men never look at you;
    And that cleans up the matter.

NEITHER BLOODY NOR BOWED

They say of me, and so they should,
It's doubtful if I come to good.
I see acquaintances and friends
Accumulating dividends,
And making enviable names
In science, art, and parlor games.
But I, despite expert advice,
Keep doing things I think are nice,
And though to good I never come—
Inseparable my nose and thumb!

THE BURNED CHILD

Love has had his way with me.
  This my heart is torn and maimed
Since he took his play with me.
  Cruel well the bow-boy aimed,

Shot, and saw the feathered shaft
  Dripping bright and bitter red.
He that shrugged his wings and laughed—
  Better had he left me dead.

Sweet, why do you plead me, then,
  Who have bled so sore of that?
Could I bear it once again? . . .
  Drop a hat, dear, drop a hat!

FIGHTING WORDS

Say my love is easy had,
    Say I'm bitten raw with pride,
Say I am too often sad—
    Still behold me at your side.

Say I'm neither brave nor young,
    Say I woo and coddle care,
Say the devil touched my tongue—
    Still you have my heart to wear.

But say my verses do not scan,
    And I get me another man!

SUNSET GUN

(1928)

GODMOTHER

The day that I was christened—
   It's a hundred years, and more!—
A hag came and listened
   At the white church door,
A-hearing her that bore me
   And all my kith and kin
Considerately, for me,
   Renouncing sin.
While some gave me corals,
   And some gave me gold,
And porringers, with morals
   Agreeably scrolled,
The hag stood, buckled
   In a dim gray cloak;
Stood there and chuckled,
   Spat, and spoke:
"There's few enough in life'll
   Be needing my help,
But I've got a trifle
   For your fine young whelp.
I give her sadness,
   And the gift of pain,
The new-moon madness,
   And the love of rain."
And little good to lave me
   In their holy silver bowl
After what she gave me—
   Rest her soul!

PARTIAL COMFORT

Whose love is given over-well
Shall look on Helen's face in hell,
Whilst they whose love is thin and wise
May view John Knox in paradise.

THE RED DRESS

I always saw, I always said
   If I were grown and free,
I'd have a gown of reddest red
   As fine as you could see,

To wear out walking, sleek and slow,
   Upon a Summer day,
And there'd be one to see me so,
   And flip the world away.

And he would be a gallant one,
   With stars behind his eyes,
And hair like metal in the sun,
   And lips too warm for lies.

I always saw us, gay and good,
   High honored in the town.
Now I am grown to womanhood. . . .
   I have the silly gown.

VICTORIA

Dear dead Victoria
    Rotted cosily;
In excelsis gloria,
    And R. I. P.

And her shroud was buttoned neat,
    And her bones were clean and round,
And her soul was at her feet
    Like a bishop's marble hound.

Albert lay a-drying,
    Lavishly arrayed,
With his soul out flying
    Where his heart had stayed.

And there's some could tell you what land
    His spirit walks serene
(But I've heard them say in Scotland
    It's never been seen).

THE COUNSELLOR

I met a man, the other day—
    A kindly man, and serious—
Who viewed me in a thoughtful way,
    And spoke me so, and spoke me thus:

"Oh, dallying's a sad mistake;
    'Tis craven to survey the morrow!
Go give your heart, and if it break—
    A wise companion is Sorrow.

"Oh, live, my child, nor keep your soul
    To crowd your coffin when you're dead." . . .
I asked his work; he dealt in coal,
    And shipped it up the Tyne, he said.

PARABLE FOR A CERTAIN VIRGIN

Oh, ponder, friend, the porcupine;
   Refresh your recollection,
And sit a moment, to define
   His means of self-protection.

How truly fortified is he!
   Where is the beast his double
In forethought of emergency
   And readiness for trouble?

Recall his figure, and his shade—
   How deftly planned and clearly
For slithering through the dappled glade
   Unseen, or pretty nearly.

Yet should an alien eye discern
   His presence in the woodland,
How little has he left to learn
   Of self-defense! My good land!

For he can run, as swift as sound,
   To where his goose may hang high;
Or thrust his head against the ground
   And tunnel half to Shanghai;

Or he can climb the dizziest bough—
   Unhesitant, mechanic—
And, resting, dash from off his brow
   The bitter beads of panic;

Or should pursuers press him hot,
  One scarcely needs to mention
His quick and cruel barbs, that got
  Shakespearean attention;

Or driven to his final ditch,
  To his extremest thicket,
He'll fight with claws and molars (which
  Is not considered cricket).

How amply armored, he, to fend
  The fear of chase that haunts him!
How well prepared our little friend!—
  And who the devil wants him?

BRIC-À-BRAC

Little things that no one needs—
　　Little things to joke about—
Little landscapes, done in beads,
　　Little morals, woven out,
Little wreaths of gilded grass,
　　Little brigs of whittled oak
Bottled painfully in glass;
　　These are made by lonely folk.

Lonely folk have lines of days
　　Long and faltering and thin;
Therefore—little wax bouquets,
　　Prayers cut upon a pin,
Little maps of pinkish lands,
　　Little charts of curly seas,
Little plats of linen strands,
　　Little verses, such as these.

INTERIOR

Her mind lives in a quiet room,
   A narrow room, and tall,
With pretty lamps to quench the gloom
   And mottoes on the wall.

There all the things are waxen neat
   And set in decorous lines;
And there are posies, round and sweet,
   And little, straightened vines.

Her mind lives tidily, apart
   From cold and noise and pain,
And bolts the door against her heart,
   Out wailing in the rain.

REUBEN'S CHILDREN

Accursed from their birth they be
Who seek to find monogamy,
Pursuing it from bed to bed—
I think they would be better dead.

FOR R. C. B.

Life comes a-hurrying,
    Or life lags slow;
But you've stopped worrying—
    Let it go!
Some call it gloomy,
    Some call it jake;
They're very little to me—
    Let them eat cake!
Some find it fair,
    Some think it hooey,
Many people care;
    But we don't, do we?

THERE WAS ONE

There was one a-riding grand
  On a tall brown mare,
And a fine gold band
  He brought me there.

A little, gold band
  He held to me
That would shine on a hand
  For the world to see.

There was one a-walking swift
  To a little, new song,
And a rose was the gift
  He carried along.

First of all the posies,
  Dewy and red.
They that have roses
  Never need bread.

There was one with a swagger
  And a soft, slow tongue,
And a bright, cold dagger
  Where his left hand swung—

Carven and gilt,
  Old and bad—
And his stroking of the hilt
  Set a girl mad.

There was one a-riding grand
    As he rode from me.
And he raised his golden band
    And he threw it in the sea.

There was one a-walking slow
    To a sad, long sigh.
And his rose drooped low,
    And he flung it down to die.

There was one with a swagger
    And a little, sharp pride,
And a bright, cold dagger
    Ever at his side.

At his side it stayed
    When he ran to part.
What is this blade
    Struck through my heart?

ON CHEATING THE FIDDLER

"Then we will have to-night!" we said.
"To-morrow—may we not be dead?"
The morrow touched our eyes; and found
Us walking firm above the ground,
Our pulses quick, our blood alight.
To-morrow's gone—we'll have to-night!

INCURABLE

And if my heart be scarred and burned,
The safer, I, for all I learned;
The calmer, I, to see it true
That ways of love are never new—
The love that sets you daft and dazed
Is every love that ever blazed;
The happier, I, to fathom this:
A kiss is every other kiss.
The reckless vow, the lovely name,
When Helen walked, were spoke the same;
The weighted breast, the grinding woe,
When Phaon fled, were ever so.
Oh, it is sure as it is sad
That any lad is every lad,
And what's a girl, to dare implore
Her dear be hers forevermore?
Though he be tried and he be bold,
And swearing death should he be cold,
He'll run the path the others went. . . .
But you, my sweet, are different.

FABLE

Oh, there once was a lady, and so I've been told,
Whose lover grew weary, whose lover grew cold.
"My child," he remarked, "though our episode ends,
In the manner of men, I suggest we be friends."
And the truest of friends ever after they were—
Oh, they lied in their teeth when they told me of her!

THE SECOND OLDEST STORY

Go I must along my ways
    Though my heart be ragged,
Dripping bitter through the days,
    Festering, and jagged.
Smile I must at every twinge,
    Kiss, to time its throbbing;
He that tears a heart to fringe
    Hates the noise of sobbing.
.   .   .   .

Weep, my love, till Heaven hears;
    Curse and moan and languish.
While I wash your wound with tears,
    Ease aloud your anguish.
Bellow of the pit in Hell
    Where you're made to linger.
There and there and well and well—
    Did he prick his finger!

A PIG'S-EYE VIEW OF LITERATURE

Byron and Shelley and Keats
Were a trio of lyrical treats.
The forehead of Shelley was cluttered with curls,
And Keats never was a descendant of earls,
And Byron walked out with a number of girls,
But it didn't impair the poetical feats
Of Byron and Shelley,
Of Byron and Shelley,
Of Byron and Shelley and Keats.

OSCAR WILDE

If, with the literate, I am
Impelled to try an epigram,
I never seek to take the credit;
We all assume that Oscar said it.

HARRIET BEECHER STOWE

The pure and worthy Mrs. Stowe
Is one we all are proud to know
As mother, wife, and authoress,—
Thank God I am content with less!

D. G. ROSSETTI

Dante Gabriel Rossetti
Buried all of his *libretti*,
Thought the matter over,—then
Went and dug them up again.

THOMAS CARLYLE

Carlyle combined the lit'ry life
With throwing teacups at his wife,
Remarking, rather testily,
"Oh, stop your dodging, Mrs. C.!"

CHARLES DICKENS

Who call him spurious and shoddy
Shall do it o'er my lifeless body.
I heartily invite such birds
To come outside and say those words!

ALEXANDRE DUMAS AND HIS SON

Although I work, and seldom cease,
At Dumas *père* and Dumas *fils*,
Alas, I cannot make me care
For Dumas *fils* and Dumas *père*.

ALFRED LORD TENNYSON

Should Heaven send me any son,
I hope he's not like Tennyson.
I'd rather have him play a fiddle
Than rise and bow and speak an idyll.

GEORGE GISSING

When I admit neglect of Gissing,
They say I don't know what I'm missing.
Until their arguments are subtler,
I think I'll stick to Samuel Butler.

WALTER SAVAGE LANDOR

Upon the work of Walter Landor
I am unfit to write with candor.
If you can read it, well and good;
But as for me, I never could.

GEORGE SAND

What time the gifted lady took
Away from paper, pen, and book,
She spent in amorous dalliance
(They do those things so well in France).

MORTAL ENEMY

Let another cross his way—
    She's the one will do the weeping!
Little need I fear he'll stray
    Since I have his heart in keeping.

Let another hail him dear—
    Little chance that he'll forget me!
Only need I curse and fear
    Her he loved before he met me.

PENELOPE

In the pathway of the sun,
In the footsteps of the breeze,
Where the world and sky are one,
   He shall ride the silver seas,
     He shall cut the glittering wave.
I shall sit at home, and rock;
Rise, to heed a neighbor's knock;
Brew my tea, and snip my thread;
Bleach the linen for my bed.
     They will call him brave.

BOHEMIA

Authors and actors and artists and such
Never know nothing, and never know much.
Sculptors and singers and those of their kidney
Tell their affairs from Seattle to Sydney.
Playwrights and poets and such horses' necks
Start off from anywhere, end up at sex.
Diarists, critics, and similar roe
Never say nothing, and never say no.
People Who Do Things exceed my endurance;
God, for a man that solicits insurance!

THE SEARCHED SOUL

When I consider, pro and con,
What things my love is built upon—
A curly mouth; a sinewed wrist;
A questioning brow; a pretty twist
Of words as old and tried as sin;
A pointed ear; a cloven chin;
Long, tapered limbs; and slanted eyes
Not cold nor kind nor darkly wise—
When so I ponder, here apart,
What shallow boons suffice my heart,
What dust-bound trivia capture me,
I marvel at my normalcy.

THE TRUSTING HEART

Oh, I'd been better dying,
　　Oh, I was slow and sad;
A fool I was, a-crying
　　About a cruel lad!

But there was one that found me,
　　That wept to see me weep,
And had his arm around me,
　　And gave me words to keep.

And I'd be better dying,
　　And I am slow and sad;
A fool I am, a-crying
　　About a tender lad!

THOUGHT FOR A SUNSHINY MORNING

It costs me never a stab nor squirm
To tread by chance upon a worm.
"Aha, my little dear," I say,
"Your clan will pay me back one day."

THE GENTLEST LADY

They say He was a serious child,
　　And quiet in his ways;
They say the gentlest lady smiled
　　To hear the neighbors' praise.

The coffers of her heart would close
　　Upon their smallest word.
Yet did they say, "How tall He grows!"
　　They thought she had not heard.

They say upon His birthday eve
　　She'd rock Him to His rest
As if she could not have Him leave
　　The shelter of her breast.

The poor must go in bitter thrift,
　　The poor must give in pain,
But ever did she set a gift
　　To greet His day again.

They say she'd kiss the boy awake,
　　And hail Him gay and clear,
But oh, her heart was like to break
　　To count another year.

THE MAID-SERVANT AT THE INN

"It's queer," she said, "I see the light
    As plain as I beheld it then,
All silver-like and calm and bright—
    We've not had stars like that again!

"And she was such a gentle thing
    To birth a baby in the cold.
The barn was dark and frightening—
    This new one's better than the old.

"I mind my eyes were full of tears,
    For I was young, and quick distressed,
But she was less than me in years
    That held a son against her breast.

"I never saw a sweeter child—
    The little one, the darling one!—
I mind I told her, when he smiled
    You'd know he was his mother's son.

"It's queer that I should see them so—
    The time they came to Bethlehem
Was more than thirty years ago;
    I've prayed that all is well with them."

FULFILMENT

For this my mother wrapped me warm,
And called me home against the storm,
And coaxed my infant nights to quiet,
And gave me roughage in my diet,
And tucked me in my bed at eight,
And clipped my hair, and marked my weight,
And watched me as I sat and stood:
That I might grow to womanhood
To hear a whistle and drop my wits
And break my heart to clattering bits.

DAYLIGHT SAVING

My answers are inadequate
To those demanding day and date,
And ever set a tiny shock
Through strangers asking what's o'clock;
Whose days are spent in whittling rhyme—
What's time to her, or she to Time?

SURPRISE

My heart went fluttering with fear
Lest you should go, and leave me here
To beat my breast and rock my head
And stretch me sleepless on my bed.
Ah, clear they see and true they say
That one shall weep, and one shall stray
For such is Love's unvarying law. . . .
I never thought, I never saw
That I should be the first to go;
How pleasant that it happened so!

SWAN SONG

First you are hot,
　　Then you are cold;
And the best you have got
　　Is the fact you are old.
Labor and hoard,
　　Worry and wed,
And the biggest reward
　　Is to die in bed.
A long time to sweat,
　　A little while to shiver;
It's all you'll get—
　　Where's the nearest river?

ON BEING A WOMAN

Why is it, when I am in Rome
I'd give an eye to be at home,
But when on native earth I be,
My soul is sick for Italy?

And why with you, my love, my lord,
Am I spectacularly bored,
Yet do you up and leave me—then
I scream to have you back again?

AFTERNOON

When I am old, and comforted,
   And done with this desire,
With Memory to share my bed
   And Peace to share my fire,

I'll comb my hair in scalloped bands
   Beneath my laundered cap,
And watch my cool and fragile hands
   Lie light upon my lap.

And I will have a sprigg'd gown
   With lace to kiss my throat;
I'll draw my curtain to the town,
   And hum a purring note.

And I'll forget the way of tears,
   And rock, and stir my tea.
But oh, I wish those blessed years
   Were further than they be!

A DREAM LIES DEAD

A dream lies dead here. May you softly go
Before this place, and turn away your eyes,
Nor seek to know the look of that which dies
Importuning Life for life. Walk not in woe,
But, for a little, let your step be slow.
And, of your mercy, be not sweetly wise
With words of hope and Spring and tenderer skies.
A dream lies dead; and this all mourners know:

Whenever one drifted petal leaves the tree—
Though white of bloom as it had been before
And proudly waitful of fecundity—
One little loveliness can be no more;
And so must Beauty bow her imperfect head
Because a dream has joined the wistful dead!

THE HOMEBODY

There still are kindly things for me to know,
Who am afraid to dream, afraid to feel—
This little chair of scrubbed and sturdy deal,
This easy book, this fire, sedate and slow.
And I shall stay with them, nor cry the woe
Of wounds across my breast that do not heal;
Nor wish that Beauty drew a duller steel,
Since I am sworn to meet her as a foe.

It may be, when the devil's own time is done,
That I shall hear the dropping of the rain
At midnight, and lie quiet in my bed;
Or stretch and straighten to the yellow sun;
Or face the turning tree, and have no pain;
So shall I learn at last my heart is dead.

SECOND LOVE

"So surely is she mine," you say, and turn
Your quick and steady mind to harder things—
To bills and bonds and talk of what men earn—
And whistle up the stair, of evenings.
And do you see a dream behind my eyes,
Or ask a simple question twice of me—
"Thus women are," you say; for men are wise
And tolerant, in their security.

How shall I count the midnights I have known
When calm you turn to me, nor feel me start,
To find my easy lips upon your own
And know my breast beneath your rhythmic heart.
Your god defer the day I tell you this:
My lad, my lad, it is not you I kiss!

FAIR WEATHER

This level reach of blue is not my sea;
Here are sweet waters, pretty in the sun,
Whose quiet ripples meet obediently
A marked and measured line, one after one.
This is no sea of mine, that humbly laves
Untroubled sands, spread glittering and warm.
I have a need of wilder, crueler waves;
They sicken of the calm, who knew the storm.

So let a love beat over me again,
Loosing its million desperate breakers wide;
Sudden and terrible to rise and wane;
Roaring the heavens apart; a reckless tide
That casts upon the heart, as it recedes,
Splinters and spars and dripping, salty weeds.

THE WHISTLING GIRL

Back of my back, they talk of me,
　　Gabble and honk and hiss;
Let them batten, and let them be—
　　Me, I can sing them this:

"Better to shiver beneath the stars,
　　Head on a faithless breast,
Than peer at the night through rusted bars,
　　And share an irksome rest.

"Better to see the dawn come up,
　　Along of a trifling one,
Than set a steady man's cloth and cup
　　And pray the day be done.

"Better be left by twenty dears
　　Than lie in a loveless bed;
Better a loaf that's wet with tears
　　Than cold, unsalted bread."

Back of my back, they wag their chins,
　　Whinny and bleat and sigh;
But better a heart a-bloom with sins
　　Than hearts gone yellow and dry!

STORY

"And if he's gone away," said she,
"Good riddance, if you're asking me.
I'm not a one to lie awake
And weep for anybody's sake.
There's better lads than him about!
I'll wear my buckled slippers out
A-dancing till the break of day.
I'm better off with him away!
And if he never come," said she,
"Now what on earth is that to me?
I wouldn't have him back!"
                              I hope
Her mother washed her mouth with soap.

FRUSTRATION

If I had a shiny gun
I could have a world of fun
Speeding bullets through the brains
Of the folk who give me pains;

Or had I some poison gas
I could make the moments pass
Bumping off a number of
People whom I do not love.

But I have no lethal weapon—
Thus does Fate our pleasure step on!
So they still are quick and well
Who should be, by rights, in hell.

HEALED

Oh, when I flung my heart away,
   The year was at its fall.
I saw my dear, the other day,
   Beside a flowering wall;
And this was all I had to say:
   "I thought that he was tall!"

LANDSCAPE

Now this must be the sweetest place
    From here to Heaven's end;
The field is white with flowering lace,
    The birches leap and bend,

The hills, beneath the roving sun,
    From green to purple pass,
And little, trifling breezes run
    Their fingers through the grass.

So good it is, so gay it is,
    So calm it is, and pure,
A one whose eyes may look on this
    Must be the happier, sure.

But me—I see it flat and gray
    And blurred with misery,
Because a lad a mile away
    Has little need of me.

POST-GRADUATE

Hope it was that tutored me,
    And Love that taught me more;
And now I learn at Sorrow's knee
    The self-same lore.

VERSES IN THE NIGHT
(AFTER AN EVENING SPENT IN READING THE BIG BOYS)

HONEYMOON

"ponder, darling, these busted statues
of yon moth-eaten forum be aware."
—E. E. CUMMINGS.

Ponder, darling, these busted statues,
    Be aware of the forum, sweet;
Feel the centuries tearing at youse—
    Don't keep asking me when we eat!

Look, my love, where the hills hang drowsy;
    Cæsar watched them, a-wondering, here.
Get yon goddesses, chipped and lousy—
    Don't be trying to bite my ear!

Child, consider the clouds above you,
    Soft and silly, like baby goats—
Don't keep asking me don't I love you!
      Judas! When will you know your oats?

TRIOLET

"Her teeth were only accidental stars
with a talent for squad drill."
—T. S. ELIOT.

Her teeth were accidental stars
With a talent for squad drill;

139

The Pleiades, Orion, Mars—
Her teeth were accidental stars,
Assured celestial corporal's bars,
    So straight they stood, and still.
Her teeth were accidental stars
    With a talent for squad drill.

MÉLANGE FOR THE UNKNOWN GEORGE

    "George is a lion. . . .
        There is no pope."
            —GERTRUDE STEIN.

    George is a lion;
        There is no pope;
    Death is the scion
        Of the house of Hope.
    George is a gazelle;
        There is no Freud;
    Charles Parnell
        Looked like Ernest Boyd.
    George is a llama;
        There is no stork;
    Papa loves Mama
        Like Jews love pork.

There's no Frances Newman—
   In a pig's right eye!
Death is as human
   As a mandrake's cry.
George is a racoon; he
   Insists there is art.
Little Annie Rooney
   Is my sweetheart.

LIEBESTOD

When I was bold, when I was bold—
    And that's a hundred years!—
Oh, never I thought my breast could hold
    The terrible weight of tears.

I said: "Now some be dolorous;
    I hear them wail and sigh,
And if it be Love that play them thus,
    Then never a love will I."

I said: "I see them rack and rue,
    I see them wring and ache,
And little I'll crack my heart in two
    With little the heart can break."

When I was gay, when I was gay—
    It's ninety years and nine!—
Oh, never I thought that Death could lay
    His terrible hand in mine.

I said: "He plies his trade among
    The musty and infirm,
A body so hard and bright and young
    Could never be meat for worm."

"I see him dull their eyes," I said,
    "And still their rattling breath.
And how under God could I be dead
    That never was meant for Death?"

But Love came by, to quench my sleep,
    And here's my sundered heart;
And bitter's my woe, and black, and deep,
    And little I guessed a part.

Yet this there is to cool my breast,
    And this to ease my spell;
Now if I were Love's, like all the rest,
    Then can I be Death's, as well.

And he shall have me, sworn and bound,
    And I'll be done with Love.
And better I'll be below the ground
    Than ever I'll be above.

FOR A FAVORITE GRAND-DAUGHTER

Never love a simple lad,
　　Guard against a wise,
Shun a timid youth and sad,
　　Hide from haunted eyes.

Never hold your heart in pain
　　For an evil-doer;
Never flip it down the lane
　　To a gifted wooer.

Never love a loving son,
　　Nor a sheep astray;
Gather up your skirts and run
　　From a tender way.

Never give away a tear,
　　Never toss and pine;
Should you heed my words, my dear,
　　You're no blood of mine!

DILEMMA

If I were mild and I were sweet,
And laid my heart before your feet,
And took my dearest thoughts to you,
And hailed your easy lies as true;
Were I to murmur "Yes," and then
"How true, my dear," and "Yes," again,
And wear my eyes discreetly down,
And tremble whitely at your frown,
And keep my words unquestioning—
My love, you'd run like anything!

Should I be frail, and I be mad,
And share my heart with every lad,
But beat my head against the floor
What times you wandered past my door;
Were I to doubt, and I to sneer,
And shriek "Farewell!" and still be here,
And break your joy, and quench your trust—
I should not see you for the dust!

THEORY

Into love and out again,
   Thus I went, and thus I go.
Spare your voice, and hold your pen—
   Well and bitterly I know
All the songs were ever sung,
   All the words were ever said;
Could it be, when I was young,
   Some one dropped me on my head?

A FAIRLY SAD TALE

I think that I shall never know
Why I am thus, and I am so.
Around me, other girls inspire
In men the rush and roar of fire,
The sweet transparency of glass,
The tenderness of April grass,
The durability of granite;
But me—I don't know how to plan it.
The lads I've met in Cupid's deadlock
Were—shall we say?—born out of wedlock.
They broke my heart, they stilled my song,
And said they had to run along,
Explaining, so to sop my tears,
First came their parents or careers.
But ever does experience
Deny me wisdom, calm, and sense!
Though she's a fool who seeks to capture
The twenty-first fine, careless rapture,
I must go on, till ends my rope,
Who from my birth was cursed with hope.
A heart in half is chaste, archaic;
But mine resembles a mosaic—
The thing's become ridiculous!
Why am I so? Why am I thus?

THE LAST QUESTION

New love, new love, where are you to lead me?
  All along a narrow way that marks a crooked line.
How are you to slake me, and how are you to feed me?
  With bitter yellow berries, and a sharp new wine.

New love, new love, shall I be forsaken?
  One shall go a-wandering, and one of us must sigh.
Sweet it is to slumber, but how shall we awaken—
  Whose will be the broken heart, when dawn comes by?

SUPERFLUOUS ADVICE

Should they whisper false of you,
  Never trouble to deny;
Should the words they say be true,
  Weep and storm and swear they lie.

DIRECTIONS FOR FINDING THE BARD

Would you see what I'm like,
    This is what to do:
Drowse and take your time, like
    Camels in a zoo.
Sit you where you are, son;
    Rest you where you lie;
I am never far, son,—
    I'll be coming by.
Watch for Trouble, walking
    All along his course,
Stepping high and stalking
    Like a funeral horse.
See his little friend, there,
    Knee beside his knee;
There's your search's end, there,—
    That'll be me!

Would you want to see me,
    This is what to try:
Stretch you, sweet and dreamy,
    Looking at the sky.
Watch for Gloom, a-wheeling
    Black across the sun,
Gibbering and squealing—
    All the crows in one.
See a little speck, there,
    Side against his side,
Sticking at his neck, there;
    Going for the ride;

Dropping, does he drop, son;
  Looping with him, maybe.
Let your seeking stop, son,—
  That'll be Baby!

BUT NOT FORGOTTEN

I think, no matter where you stray,
That I shall go with you a way.
Though you may wander sweeter lands,
You will not soon forget my hands,
Nor yet the way I held my head,
Nor all the tremulous things I said.
You still will see me, small and white
And smiling, in the secret night,
And feel my arms about you when
The day comes fluttering back again.
I think, no matter where you be,
You'll hold me in your memory
And keep my image, there without me,
By telling later loves about me.

TWO-VOLUME NOVEL

The sun's gone dim, and
    The moon's turned black;
For I loved him, and
    He didn't love back.

POUR PRENDRE CONGÉ

I'm sick of embarking in dories
   Upon an emotional sea.
I'm wearied of playing Dolores
   (A rôle never written for me).

I'll never again like a cub lick
   My wounds while I squeal at the hurt.
No more I'll go walking in public,
   My heart hanging out of my shirt.

I'm tired of entwining me garlands
   Of weather-worn hemlock and bay.
I'm over my longing for far lands—
   I wouldn't give *that* for Cathay.

I'm through with performing the ballet
   Of love unrequited and told.
Euterpe, I tender you *vale;*
   Good-bye, and take care of that cold.

I'm done with this burning and giving
   And reeling the rhymes of my woes.
And how I'll be making my living,
   The Lord in His mystery knows.

FOR A LADY WHO MUST WRITE VERSE

Unto seventy years and seven,
  Hide your double birthright well—
You, that are the brat of Heaven
  And the pampered heir to Hell.

Let your rhymes be tinsel treasures,
  Strung and seen and thrown aside.
Drill your apt and docile measures
  Sternly as you drill your pride.

Show your quick, alarming skill in
  Tidy mockeries of art;
Never, never dip your quill in
  Ink that rushes from your heart.

When your pain must come to paper,
  See it dust, before the day;
Let your night-light curl and caper,
  Let it lick the words away.

Never print, poor child, a lay on
  Love and tears and anguishing,
Lest a cooled, benignant Phaon
  Murmur, "Silly little thing!"

RHYME AGAINST LIVING

If wild my breast and sore my pride,
I bask in dreams of suicide;
If cool my heart and high my head,
I think, "How lucky are the dead!"

WISDOM

This I say, and this I know:
   Love has seen the last of me.
Love's a trodden lane to woe,
   Love's a path to misery.

This I know, and knew before,
   This I tell you, of my years:
Hide your heart, and lock your door.
   Hell's afloat in lovers' tears.

Give your heart, and toss and moan,
   What a pretty fool you look!
I am sage, who sit alone;
   Here's my wool, and here's my book.

Look! A lad's a-waiting there,
   Tall he is and bold, and gay.
What the devil do I care
   What I know, and what I say?

CODA

There's little in taking or giving,
   There's little in water or wine;
This living, this living, this living
   Was never a project of mine.
Oh, hard is the struggle, and sparse is
   The gain of the one at the top,
For art is a form of catharsis,
   And love is a permanent flop,
And work is the province of cattle,
   And rest's for a clam in a shell,
So I'm thinking of throwing the battle—
   Would you kindly direct me to hell?

DEATH AND TAXES

(1931)

PRAYER FOR A PRAYER

Dearest one, when I am dead
  Never seek to follow me.
    Never mount the quiet hill
    Where the copper leaves are still,
  As my heart is, on the tree
Standing at my narrow bed.

Only, of your tenderness,
  Pray a little prayer at night.
    Say: "I have forgiven now—
    I, so weak and sad; O Thou,
  Wreathed in thunder, robed in light,
Surely Thou wilt do no less."

AFTER A SPANISH PROVERB

Oh, mercifullest one of all,
    Oh, generous as dear,
None lived so lowly, none so small,
    Thou couldst withhold thy tear;

How swift, in pure compassion,
    How meek in charity,
To offer friendship to the one
    Who begged but love of thee!

Oh, gentle word, and sweetest said!
    Oh, tender hand, and first
To hold the warm, delicious bread
    To lips burned black of thirst.

THE FLAW IN PAGANISM

Drink and dance and laugh and lie,
    Love, the reeling midnight through,
For tomorrow we shall die!
    (But, alas, we never do.)

THE DANGER OF WRITING DEFIANT VERSE

And now I have another lad!
   No longer need you tell
How all my nights are slow and sad
   For loving you too well.

His ways are not your wicked ways,
   He's not the like of you.
He treads his path of reckoned days,
   A sober man, and true.

They'll never see him in the town,
   Another on his knee.
He'd cut his laden orchards down,
   If that would pleasure me.

He'd give his blood to paint my lips
   If I should wish them red.
He prays to touch my finger-tips
   Or stroke my prideful head.

He never weaves a glinting lie,
   Or brags the hearts he'll keep.
I have forgotten how to sigh—
   Remembered how to sleep.

He's none to kiss away my mind—
   A slower way is his.
Oh, Lord! On reading this, I find
   A silly lot he is.

DISTANCE

Were you to cross the world, my dear,
    To work or love or fight,
I could be calm and wistful here,
    And close my eyes at night.

It were a sweet and gallant pain
    To be a sea apart;
But, oh, to have you down the lane
    Is bitter to my heart.

THE EVENING PRIMROSE

You know the bloom, unearthly white,
That none has seen by morning light—
The tender moon, alone, may bare
Its beauty to the secret air.
Who'd venture past its dark retreat
Must kneel, for holy things and sweet.
That blossom, mystically blown,
No man may gather for his own
Nor touch it, lest it droop and fall. . . .
Oh, I am not like that at all!

SANCTUARY

My land is bare of chattering folk;
    The clouds are low along the ridges,
And sweet's the air with curly smoke
    From all my burning bridges.

CHERRY WHITE

I never see that prettiest thing—
A cherry bough gone white with Spring—
But what I think, "How gay 'twould be
To hang me from a flowering tree."

SALOME'S DANCING-LESSON

She that begs a little boon
   (Heel and toe! Heel and toe!)
Little gets—and nothing, soon.
   (No, no, no! No, no, no!)
She that calls for costly things
Priceless finds her offerings—
What's impossible to kings?
   (Heel and toe! Heel and toe!)

Kings are shaped as other men.
   (Step and turn! Step and turn!)
Ask what none may ask again.
   (Will you learn? Will you learn?)
Lovers whine, and kisses pall,
Jewels tarnish, kingdoms fall—
Death's the rarest prize of all!
   (Step and turn! Step and turn!)

Veils are woven to be dropped.
   (One, two, three! One, two, three!)
Aging eyes are slowest stopped.
   (Quietly! Quietly!)
She whose body's young and cool
Has no need of dancing-school—
Scratch a king and find a fool!
   (One, two, three! One, two, three!)

MY OWN

Then let them point my every tear,
    And let them mock and moan;
Another week, another year,
    And I'll be with my own

Who slumber now by night and day
    In fields of level brown;
Whose hearts within their breasts were clay
    Before they laid them down.

SOLACE

There was a rose that faded young;
I saw its shattered beauty hung
  Upon a broken stem.
I heard them say, "What need to care
With roses budding everywhere?"
  I did not answer them.

There was a bird, brought down to die;
They said, "A hundred fill the sky—
  What reason to be sad?"
There was a girl, whose lover fled;
I did not wait, the while they said,
  "There's many another lad."

LITTLE WORDS

When you are gone, there is nor bloom nor leaf,
   Not singing sea at night, nor silver birds;
And I can only stare, and shape my grief
   In little words.

I cannot conjure loveliness, to drown
   The bitter woe that racks my cords apart.
The weary pen that sets my sorrow down
   Feeds at my heart.

There is no mercy in the shifting year,
   No beauty wraps me tenderly about.
I turn to little words—so you, my dear,
   Can spell them out.

ORNITHOLOGY FOR BEGINNERS

The bird that feeds from off my palm
Is sleek, affectionate, and calm,
But double, to me, is worth the thrush
A-flickering in the elder bush.

TOMBSTONES IN THE STARLIGHT

I. THE MINOR POET

His little trills and chirpings were his best.
  No music like the nightingale's was born
Within his throat; but he, too, laid his breast
  Upon a thorn.

II. THE PRETTY LADY

She hated bleak and wintry things alone.
  All that was warm and quick, she loved too well—
A light, a flame, a heart against her own;
  It is forever bitter cold, in Hell.

III. THE VERY RICH MAN

He'd have the best, and that was none too good;
  No barrier could hold, before his terms.
He lies below, correct in cypress wood,
  And entertains the most exclusive worms.

IV. THE FISHERWOMAN

The man she had was kind and clean
  And well enough for every day,
But, oh, dear friends, you should have seen
  The one that got away!

V. THE CRUSADER

Arrived in Heaven, when his sands were run,
    He seized a quill, and sat him down to tell
The local press that something should be done
    About that noisy nuisance, Gabriel.

VI. THE ACTRESS

Her name, cut clear upon this marble cross,
    Shines, as it shone when she was still on earth;
While tenderly the mild, agreeable moss
    Obscures the figures of her date of birth.

THE LITTLE OLD LADY IN LAVENDER SILK

I was seventy-seven, come August,
    I shall shortly be losing my bloom;
I've experienced zephyr and raw gust
    And (symbolical) flood and simoom.

When you come to this time of abatement,
    To this passing from summer to fall,
It is manners to issue a statement
    As to what you got out of it all.

So I'll say, though reflection unnerves me
    And pronouncements I dodge as I can,
That I think (if my memory serves me)
    There was nothing more fun than a man!

In my youth, when the crescent was too wan
    To embarrass with beams from above,
By the aid of some local Don Juan
    I fell into the habit of love.

And I learned how to kiss and be merry—an
    Education left better unsung.
My neglect of the waters Pierian
    Was a scandal, when Grandma was young.

Though the shabby unbalanced the splendid,
    And the bitter outmeasured the sweet,
I should certainly do as I then did,
    Were I given the chance to repeat.

For contrition is hollow and wraithful,
   And regret is no part of my plan,
And I think (if my memory's faithful)
   There was nothing more fun than a man!

GARDEN-SPOT

God's acre was her garden-spot, she said;
   She sat there often, of the summer days,
Little and slim and sweet, among the dead,
   Her hair a fable in the leveled rays.

She turned the fading wreath, the rusted cross,
   And knelt to coax about the wiry stem.
I see her gentle fingers on the moss
   Now it is anguish to remember them.

And once I saw her weeping, when she rose
   And walked a way and turned to look around—
The quick and envious tears of one that knows
   She shall not lie in consecrated ground.

VERS DÉMODÉ

For one, the amaryllis and the rose;
   The poppy, sweet as never lilies are;
The ripen'd vine, that beckons as it blows;
   The dancing star.

For one, the trodden rosemary and rue;
   The bowl, dipt ever in the purple stream.
And, for the other one, a fairer due—
   Sleep, and no dream.

SONNET FOR THE END OF A SEQUENCE

So take my vows and scatter them to sea;
Who swears the sweetest is no more than human.
And say no kinder words than these of me:
"Ever she longed for peace, but was a woman!
And thus they are, whose silly female dust
Needs little enough to clutter it and bind it,
Who meet a slanted gaze, and ever must
Go build themselves a soul to dwell behind it."

For now I am my own again, my friend!
This scar but points the whiteness of my breast;
This frenzy, like its betters, spins an end,
And now I am my own. And that is best.
Therefore, I am immeasurably grateful
To you, for proving shallow, false and hateful.

IN THE MEADOW

The buttercups that brushed my knee
Their golden dreams have whispered me,
But how am I to murmur back,
For gold is lovelier than black?

THE APPLE TREE

When first we saw the apple tree
    The boughs were dark and straight,
But never grief to give had we,
    Though Spring delayed so late.

When last I came away from there
    The boughs were heavy hung,
But little grief had I to spare
    For Summer, perished young.

ISEULT OF BRITTANY

So delicate my hands, and long,
    They might have been my pride.
And there were those to make them song
    Who for their touch had died.

Too frail to cup a heart within,
    Too soft to hold the free—
How long these lovely hands have been
    A bitterness to me!

"STAR LIGHT, STAR BRIGHT—"

Star, that gives a gracious dole,
    What am I to choose?
Oh, will it be a shriven soul,
    Or little buckled shoes?

Shall I wish a wedding-ring,
    Bright and thin and round,
Or plead you send me covering—
    A newly spaded mound?

Gentle beam, shall I implore
    Gold, or sailing-ships,
Or beg I hate forevermore
    A pair of lying lips?

Swing you low or high away,
    Burn you hot or dim;
My only wish I dare not say—
    Lest you should grant me him.

THE SEA

Who lay against the sea, and fled,
  Who lightly loved the wave,
Shall never know, when he is dead,
  A cool and murmurous grave.

But in a shallow pit shall rest
  For all eternity,
And bear the earth upon the breast
  That once had worn the sea.

GUINEVERE AT HER FIRESIDE

A nobler king had never breath—
   I say it now, and said it then.
Who weds with such is wed till death
   And wedded stays in Heaven. Amen.

(And oh, the shirts of linen-lawn,
   And all the armor, tagged and tied,
And church on Sundays, dusk and dawn,
   And bed a thing to kneel beside!)

The bravest one stood tall above
   The rest, and watched me as a light.
I heard and heard them talk of love;
   I'd naught to do but think, at night.

The bravest man has littlest brains;
   That chalky fool from Astolat
With all her dying and her pains!—
   Thank God, I helped him over that.

I found him not unfair to see—
   I like a man with peppered hair!
And thus it came about. Ah, me,
   Tristram was busied otherwhere. . . .

A nobler king had never breath—
   I say it now, and said it then.
Who weds with such is wed till death
   And wedded stays in Heaven. Amen.

TRANSITION

Too long and quickly have I lived to vow
   The woe that stretches me shall never wane,
   Too often seen the end of endless pain
To swear that peace no more shall cool my brow.
I know, I know—again the shriveled bough
   Will burgeon sweetly in the gentle rain,
   And these hard lands be quivering with grain—
I tell you only: it is Winter now.

What if I know, before the Summer goes
Where dwelt this bitter frenzy shall be rest?
What is it now, that June shall surely bring
New promise, with the swallow and the rose?
My heart is water, that I first must breast
The terrible, slow loveliness of Spring.

LINES ON READING TOO MANY POETS

Roses, rooted warm in earth,
    Bud in rhyme, another age;
Lilies know a ghostly birth
    Strewn along a patterned page;
Golden lad and chimbley sweep
Die; and so their song shall keep.

Wind that in Arcadia starts
    In and out a couplet plays;
And the drums of bitter hearts
    Beat the measure of a phrase.
Sweets and woes but come to print
Quae cum ita sint.

BALLADE OF UNFORTUNATE MAMMALS

Love is sharper than stones or sticks;
  Lone as the sea, and deeper blue;
Loud in the night as a clock that ticks;
  Longer-lived than the Wandering Jew.
Show me a love was done and through,
  Tell me a kiss escaped its debt!
Son, to your death you'll pay your due—
  Women and elephants never forget.

Ever a man, alas, would mix,
  Ever a man, heigh-ho, must woo;
So he's left in the world-old fix,
  Thus is furthered the sale of rue,
Son, your chances are thin and few—
  Won't you ponder, before you're set?
Shoot if you must, but hold in view
  Women and elephants never forget.

Down from Caesar past Joynson-Hicks
  Echoes the warning, ever new:
Though they're trained to amusing tricks,
  Gentler, they, than the pigeon's coo,
Careful, son, of the cursèd two—
  Either one is a dangerous pet;
Natural history proves it true—
  Women and elephants never forget.

L'Envoi:
Prince, a precept I'd leave for you,
    Coined in Eden, existing yet:
Skirt the parlor, and shun the zoo—
    Women and elephants never forget.

FROM A LETTER FROM LESBIA

... So, praise the gods, at last he's away!
  And let me tend you this advice, my dear:
Take any lover that you will, or may,
  Except a poet. All of them are queer.

It's just the same—a quarrel or a kiss
  Is but a tune to play upon his pipe.
He's always hymning that or wailing this;
  Myself, I much prefer the business type.

That thing he wrote, the time the sparrow died—
  (Oh, most unpleasant—gloomy, tedious words!)
I called it sweet, and made believe I cried;
  The stupid fool! I've always hated birds. ...

PURPOSELY UNGRAMMATICAL LOVE SONG

There's many and many, and not so far,
   Is willing to dry my tears away;
There's many to tell me what you are,
   And never a lie to all they say.

It's little the good to hide my head,
   It's never the use to bar my door;
There's many as counts the tears I shed,
   There's mourning hearts for my heart is sore.

There's honester eyes than your blue eyes,
   There's better a mile than such as you.
But when did I say that I was wise,
   And when did I hope that you were true?

PRAYER FOR A NEW MOTHER

The things she knew, let her forget again—
    The voices in the sky, the fear, the cold,
The gaping shepherds, and the queer old men
    Piling their clumsy gifts of foreign gold.

Let her have laughter with her little one;
    Teach her the endless, tuneless songs to sing;
Grant her her right to whisper to her son
    The foolish names one dare not call a king.

Keep from her dreams the rumble of a crowd,
    The smell of rough-cut wood, the trail of red,
The thick and chilly whiteness of the shroud
    That wraps the strange new body of the dead.

Ah, let her go, kind Lord, where mothers go
    And boast his pretty words and ways, and plan
The proud and happy years that they shall know
    Together, when her son is grown a man.

MIDNIGHT

The stars are soft as flowers, and as near;
    The hills are webs of shadow, slowly spun;
No separate leaf or single blade is here—
    All blend to one.

No moonbeam cuts the air; a sapphire light
    Rolls lazily, and slips again to rest.
There is no edgèd thing in all this night,
    Save in my breast.

NINON DE L'ENCLOS,
ON HER LAST BIRTHDAY

So let me have the rouge again,
   And comb my hair the curly way.
The poor young men, the dear young men—
   They'll all be here by noon today.

And I shall wear the blue, I think—
   They beg to touch its rippled lace;
Or do they love me best in pink,
   So sweetly flattering the face?

And are you sure my eyes are bright,
   And is it true my cheek is clear?
Young what's-his-name stayed half the night;
   He vows to cut his throat, poor dear!

So bring my scarlet slippers, then,
   And fetch the powder-puff to me.
The dear young men, the poor young men—
   They think I'm only seventy!

ULTIMATUM

I'm wearied of wearying love, my friend,
 Of worry and strain and doubt;
Before we begin, let us view the end,
 And maybe I'll do without.
There's never the pang that was worth the tear,
 And toss in the night I won't—
So either you do or you don't, my dear,
 Either you do or you don't!

The table is ready, so lay your cards
 And if they should augur pain,
I'll tender you ever my kind regards
 And run for the fastest train.
I haven't the will to be spent and sad;
 My heart's to be gay and true—
Then either you don't or you do, my lad,
 Either you don't or you do!

OF A WOMAN, DEAD YOUNG

(J. H., 1905–1930)

If she had been beautiful, even,
Or wiser than women about her,
Or had moved with a certain defiance;
If she had had sons at her sides,
And she with her hands on their shoulders,
Sons, to make troubled the Gods—
But where was there wonder in her?
What had she, better or eviler,
Whose days were a pattering of peas
From the pod to the bowl in her lap?

That the pine tree is blasted by lightning,
And the bowlder split raw from the mountain,
And the river dried short in its rushing—
That I can know, and be humble.
But that They who have trodden the stars
Should turn from Their echoing highway
To trample a daisy, unnoticed
In a field full of small, open flowers—
Where is Their triumph in that?
Where is Their pride, and Their vengeance?

THE WILLOW

On sweet young earth where the myrtle presses,
    Long we lay, when the May was new;
The willow was winding the moon in her tresses,
    The bud of the rose was told with dew.

And now on the brittle ground I'm lying,
    Screaming to die with the dead year's dead;
The stem of the rose is black and drying,
    The willow is tossing the wind from her head.

BALLADE OF A TALKED-OFF EAR

Daily I listen to wonder and woe,
Nightly I hearken to knave or to ace,
Telling me stories of lava and snow,
Delicate fables of ribbon and lace,
Tales of the quarry, the kill, the chase,
Longer than heaven and duller than hell—
Never you blame me, who cry my case:
"Poets alone should kiss and tell!"

Dumbly I hear what I never should know,
Gently I counsel of pride and of grace;
Into minutiæ gayly they go,
Telling the name and the time and the place.
Cede them your silence and grant them space—
Who tenders an inch shall be raped of an ell!
Sympathy's ever the boaster's brace;
Poets alone should kiss and tell.

Why am I tithed what I never did owe?
Choked with vicarious saffron and mace?
Weary my lids, and my fingers are slow—
Gentlemen, damn you, you've halted my pace.
Only the lads of the cursèd race,
Only the knights of the desolate spell,
May point me the lines the blood-drops trace—
Poets alone should kiss and tell.

L'Envoi:
Prince or commoner, tenor or bass,
Painter or plumber or never-do-well,
Do me a favor and shut your face—
Poets alone should kiss and tell.

SONNET ON AN ALPINE NIGHT

My hand, a little raised, might press a star;
Where I may look, the frosted peaks are spun,
So shaped before Olympus was begun,
Spanned each to each, now, by a silver bar.
Thus to face Beauty have I traveled far,
But now, as if around my heart were run
Hard, lacing fingers, so I stand undone.
Of all my tears, the bitterest these are.

Who humbly followed Beauty all her ways,
Begging the brambles that her robe had passed,
Crying her name in corridors of stone,
That day shall know his weariedest of days—
When Beauty, still and suppliant at last,
Does not suffice him, once they are alone.

REQUIESCAT

Tonight my love is sleeping cold
 Where none may see and none shall pass.
The daisies quicken in the mould,
 And richer fares the meadow grass.

The warding cypress pleads the skies,
 The mound goes level in the rain.
My love all cold and silent lies—
 Pray God it will not rise again!

SWEET VIOLETS

You are brief and frail and blue—
Little sisters, I am, too.
You are heaven's masterpieces—
Little loves, the likeness ceases.

PROLOGUE TO A SAGA

Maidens, gather not the yew,
    Leave the glossy myrtle sleeping;
Any lad was born untrue,
    Never a one is fit your weeping.

Pretty dears, your tumult cease;
    Love's a fardel, burthening double.
Clear your hearts, and have you peace—
    Gangway, girls: I'll show you trouble.

SUMMARY

Every love's the love before
    In a duller dress.
That's the measure of my lore—
    Here's my bitterness:
Would I knew a little more,
    Or very much less!

DEATH AND TAXES
AND OTHER POEMS

(1936)

SIGHT

Unseemly are the open eyes
    That watch the midnight sheep,
That look upon the secret skies
    Nor close, abashed, in sleep;

That see the dawn drag in, unbidden,
    To birth another day—
Oh, better far their gaze were hidden
    Below the decent clay.

THE LADY'S REWARD

Lady, lady, never start
Conversation toward your heart;
Keep your pretty words serene;
Never murmur what you mean.
Show yourself, by word and look,
Swift and shallow as a brook.
Be as cool and quick to go
As a drop of April snow;
Be as delicate and gay
As a cherry flower in May.
Lady, lady, never speak
Of the tears that burn your cheek—
She will never win him, whose
Words had shown she feared to lose.
Be you wise and never sad,
You will get your lovely lad.
Never serious be, nor true,
And your wish will come to you—
And if that makes you happy, kid,
You'll be the first it ever did.

PRISONER

Long I fought the driving lists,
　　Plume a-stream and armor clanging;
Link on link, between my wrists,
　　Now my heavy freedom's hanging.

TEMPS PERDU

I never may turn the loop of a road
   Where sudden, ahead, the sea is lying,
But my heart drags down with an ancient load—
   My heart, that a second before was flying.

I never behold the quivering rain—
   And sweeter the rain than a lover to me—
But my heart is wild in my breast with pain;
   My heart, that was tapping contentedly.

There's never a rose spreads new at my door
   Nor a strange bird crosses the moon at night
But I know I have known its beauty before,
   And a terrible sorrow along with the sight.

The look of a laurel tree birthed for May
   Or a sycamore bared for a new November
Is as old and as sad as my furtherest day—
   What is it, what is it, I almost remember?

AUTUMN VALENTINE

In May my heart was breaking—
   Oh, wide the wound, and deep!
And bitter it beat at waking,
   And sore it split in sleep.

And when it came November,
   I sought my heart, and sighed,
"Poor thing, do you remember?"
   "What heart was that?" it cried.

THE PORTABLE

DOROTHY PARKER

(1944)

WAR SONG

Soldier, in a curious land
   All across a swaying sea,
Take her smile and lift her hand—
   Have no guilt of me.

Soldier, when were soldiers true?
   If she's kind and sweet and gay,
Use the wish I send to you—
   Lie not lone till day!

Only, for the nights that were,
   Soldier, and the dawns that came,
When in sleep you turn to her
   Call her by my name.

1944

POEMS UNCOLLECTED BY PARKER

ANY PORCH

"I'm reading that new thing of Locke's—
　　So whimsical, isn't he? Yes—"
"My dear, have you seen those new smocks?
　　They're nightgowns—no more, and no less."

"I don't call Mrs. Brown *bad*,
　　She's *un*-moral, dear, not *im*moral—"
"Well, really, it makes me so mad
　　To think what I paid for that coral!"

"My husband says, often, 'Elise,
　　You feel things too deeply, you do—' "
"Yes, forty a month, if you please,
　　Oh, servants impose on *me*, too."

"I don't want the vote for myself,
　　But women with property, dear—"
"I think the poor girl's on the shelf,
　　She's talking about her 'career.' "

"This war's such a frightful affair,
　　I know for a fact, that in France—"
"I love Mrs. Castle's bobbed hair;
　　They say that *he* taught her to dance."

"I've heard I was psychic, before,
　　To think that you saw it—how funny—"
"Why, he must be sixty, or more,
　　I told you she'd marry for money!"

213

"I really look thinner, you say?
    I've lost all my hips? Oh, you're *sweet*—"
"Imagine the city to-day!
    Humidity's *much* worse than heat!"

"You never could guess, from my face,
    The bundle of nerves that I am—"
"If you had led off with your ace,
    They'd never have gotten that slam."

"So she's got the children? That's true;
    The fault was most certainly his—"
"You know the de Peysters? You *do*?
    My *dear*, what a small world this is!"

THE BRIDGE FIEND

How do we cut for the deal?
　　That's so, we did it before.
Partner, we'll beat them, I feel—
　　Oh, I just hate keeping score!
Really, I don't understand,
　　Under the line or above?
Partner, just *look* at my hand!
　　I must be lucky at love.

Partner, I haven't a thing—
　　The hearts were dealt in a lump.
Don't tell me that was *your* king—
　　Well, then, I've wasted a trump.
Now it's my bid, I suppose—
　　Goodness, who dealt me this mess?
You made it lilies on *those?*
　　Isn't it time to progress!

Oh, did you see what you did?
　　Why, you're an absolute dub!
Didn't you hear what I bid?
　　Couldn't you lead me a club?
Kindly keep track of what's played—
　　What a remarkable lead!
Tell me how many we made—
　　Set us three hundred? Indeed!

A MUSICAL COMEDY THOUGHT

My heart is fairly melting at the thought of Julian Eltinge;
  His vice versa, Vesta Tilley, too.
Our language is so dexterous, let us call them ambi-sexterous—
  Why hasn't this occurred before to you?

WOMEN

A HATE SONG

I hate Women;
They get on my nerves.

There are the Domestic ones.
They are the worst.
Every moment is packed with Happiness.
They breathe deeply
And walk with large strides, eternally hurrying home
To see about dinner.
They are the kind
Who say, with a tender smile, "Money's not everything."
They are always confronting me with dresses,
Saying, "I made this myself."
They read Woman's pages and try out the recipes.
Oh, how I hate that kind of woman.

Then there are the human Sensitive Plants;
The Bundles of Nerves.
They are different from everybody else; they even tell you so.
Someone is always stepping on their feelings.
Everything hurts them—deeply.
Their eyes are forever filling with tears.
They always want to talk to me about the Real Things,
The things that Matter.
Yes, they know they could write.
Conventions stifle them.
They are always longing to get away—Away from It All!
—I wish to Heaven they would.

And then there are those who are always in Trouble.
Always.
Usually they have Husband-trouble.
They are Wronged.
They are the women whom nobody—understands.
They wear faint, wistful smiles.
And, when spoken to, they start.
They begin by saying they must suffer in silence.
No one will ever know—
And then they go into details.

Then there are the Well-Informed ones.
They are pests.
They know everything on earth
And will tell you about it gladly.
They feel it their mission to correct wrong impressions
They know Dates and Middle names.
They absolutely ooze Current Events.
Oh, how they bore me.

There are the ones who simply cannot Fathom
Why all the men are mad about them.
They say they've tried and tried.
They tell you about someone's husband;
What he said
And how he looked when he said it.
And then they sigh and ask,
"My dear, what is there about me?"
—Don't you hate them?

There are the unfailingly Cheerful ones.
They are usually unmarried.
They are always busy making little Gifts
And planning little surprises.
They tell me to be, like them, always looking on the Bright Side.
They ask me what they would do without their sense of humor?
I sometimes yearn to kill them.
Any jury would acquit me.

I hate Women;
They get on my nerves.

THE GUNMAN AND THE DÉBUTANTE

A MORAL TALE

A wild and wicked gunman—one who held a gang in thrall—
   A menace to the lives of me and you,
Was counting up, exultingly, the day's successful haul—
   As gunmen are extremely apt to do.
A string of pearls, a watch or two, a roll of bills, a ring,
   Some pocketbooks—about a dozen, say—
An emerald tiara—oh, a very pretty thing!
   Yes, really, quite a gratifying day.

A dainty little débutante came trippingly along,
   With wistful, trusting eyes of baby blue;
She softly hummed a fragment of a most Parisian song—
   As débutantes are very apt to do.
That wild and wicked gunman felt he couldn't miss the chance
   To end his busy day triumphantly;
"Though scarcely in the habit of attacking débutantes,
   Your money or your life, my dear," said he.

The dainty little débutante was trembling with alarm,
   Appealingly she looked him through and through,
And laid her helpless little hand upon his brawny arm—
   As débutantes are very apt to do.
Then earnestly she prayed the wicked gunman to be good,
   She begged that he'd reform that very day;
Until he dropped his wicked gun, and promised that he would,
   And bade her go her sweet and harmless way.

The wild and wicked gunman sat considering it all.
  "At last," he cried, "I've met my Waterloo";
He vowed he'd give to charity the day's successful haul—
  As gunmen are extremely apt to do.
But when he tried to find his gains and give to those in want—
  The pocketbooks, the watches, bills and ring—
He found, to his amazement, that the little débutante
  Had taken every solitary thing!

THE LADY IN BACK

I don't know what her name is, for you see we've never met;
    I don't know if she's dark, or if she's fair;
I don't know if she's young or old, or rich or poor—and yet
    Whatever place I chance to go, she's there.
I don't know where she came from, and I don't know where
      she'll go;
    Why fate has linked our lives I cannot see,
The world's so full of people—oh, I'd really like to know
    Why must she *always* sit in back of me?

She's always right on duty when I go to see a play—
    Unfailingly, she's seen that play before,
And so she tells what's coming, in her entertaining way—
    For me, the drama holds surprise no more.
"Now watch, the husband enters, as I told you that he would,
    At first you'll think he'll shoot her, but he'll not.
And later she goes back to him, and says that she'll be good"—
    Obligingly she thus unfolds the plot.

When I am at the opera, of course she's sure to come.
    She there adopts another policy—
The more familiar arias she feels obliged to hum,
    And always just a trifle off the key.
But when the singers reach those heights to which she can not
      climb—
    Oh, then I plumb the very depths of gloom!
For, lest I be too happy, she will occupy that time
    By long accounts of who's in love with whom.

I never can avoid her at the humble picture show,
    Of course, the film is always one she's seen
Reliable as Mary's lamb, she's right behind, I know,
    Revealing all the secrets of the screen.
When heroes tumble over cliffs, as movie heroes will,
    And villains blow up bridges, just for fun,
I know that she takes pleasure in extinguishing my thrill
    By telling just exactly how it's done.

I really couldn't tell you if she's widow, maid, or wife;
    I've never heard about her family;
I don't know who appointed her to take the joy from life,
    I can't imagine what she sees in me.
I often sit and think of it, and wonder why it's so,
    Why, every place that I am, she is too,
The whole wide world to choose from—oh, I'd really like to
        know
    Why can't she *sometimes* sit in back of you?

MEN

A HATE SONG

I hate Men;
They irritate me.

I

There are the Serious Thinkers—
There ought to be a law against them.
They see life, as through shell-rimmed glasses, darkly.
They are always drawing their weary hands
Across their wan brows.
They talk about Humanity
As if they had just invented it;
They have to keep helping it along.
They revel in strikes
And they are eternally getting up petitions.
They are doing a wonderful thing for the Great Unwashed—
They are living right down among them.
They can hardly wait
For "The Masses" to appear on the newsstands,
And they read all those Russian novels—
The sex best sellers.

II

There are the Cave Men—
The Specimens of Red-Blooded Manhood.

They eat everything very rare,
They are scarcely ever out of their cold baths,
And they want everybody to feel their muscles.
They talk in loud voices,
Using short Anglo-Saxon words.
They go around raising windows,
And they slap people on the back,
And tell them what they need is exercise.
They are always just on the point of walking to San Francisco,
Or crossing the ocean in a sailboat,
Or going through Russia on a sled—
I wish to God they would!

III

And then there are the Sensitive Souls
Who do interior decorating, for Art's sake.
They always smell faintly of vanilla
And put drops of sandalwood on their cigarettes.
They are continually getting up costume balls
So that they can go
As something out of the "Arabian Nights."
They give studio teas
Where people sit around on cushions
And wish they hadn't come.
They look at a woman languorously, through half-closed eyes,
And tell her, in low, passionate tones,
What she ought to wear.

Color is everything to them—everything;
The wrong shade of purple
Gives them a nervous breakdown.

IV

Then there are the ones
Who are Simply Steeped in Crime.
They tell you how they haven't been to bed
For four nights.
They frequent those dramas
Where the only good lines
Are those of the chorus.
They stagger from one cabaret to another,
And they give you the exact figures of their gambling debts.
They hint darkly at the terrible part
That alcohol plays in their lives.
And then they shake their heads
And say Heaven must decide what is going to become of them—
I wish I were Heaven!

I hate Men;
They irritate me.

ACTRESSES

A HATE SONG

I hate Actresses;
They get on my nerves.

There are the Adventuresses,
The Ladies with Lavender Pasts.
They wear gowns that show all their emotions,
And they simply can't stop undulating.
The only stage properties they require
Are a box of cigarettes and a package of compromising letters.
Their Big Scene invariably takes place in the hero's apartment.
They are always hanging around behind screens
And overhearing things about the heroine.
They go around clutching their temples
And saying, Would to God they were good—
Would to God they were!

There are the Wronged Ones;
The Girls Whose Mothers Never Told Them.
In the first act they wear pink gingham sunbonnets
And believe implicitly in the stork.
In the third act they are clad in somber black
And know that there isn't any Santa Claus.
They are always going out into the night.
They faint a great deal,
And if anyone lets them get near the center of the stage
They immediately burst into hysterics.
They unfortunately never commit suicide until the last act—
It's always the audience that pays and pays and pays.

Then there are the Musical Comedy Stars;
The press-agent's livelihood.
They sing about love—in waltz time—
And they dance as if something were just about to break.
They end by appearing in a piece of court plaster
And an American flag,
And then the audience has to stand up.
The show isn't considered a success
Until they climb into a flower-wreathed swing,
And swing far out, over the orchestra—
Oh, that I might be there when the ropes break.

And there are the Emotional Ones;
The ones who say,
"I'll have two lumps of sugar in my tea, please,"
In exactly the same tones as they say
"Yes, it was I who murdered him."
They are forever tearing their hair—
I hope it hurts them.
They shriek at everything,
Usually at the hero,
And they hurl themselves on the floor at his feet
And say that they wish it were all over—
They said something.

Then there are the child Actresses
Who should be unseen and not heard.

They go around telling people about Heaven
As if they were special correspondents.
They are always climbing up on innocent bystanders
And asking them why they look so sad;
They eternally bring their fathers and mothers together,
Which is always an error of judgment.
They never fail to appear in their nightgowns
And then kneel down beside the orchestra leader,
And say their prayers to the spotlight man—
I wish I were Commodore Gerry.

I hate Actresses;
They get on my nerves.

RELATIVES

A HATE SONG

I hate Relatives;
They cramp my style.

There are Aunts.
Even the best of us have them.
They are always dropping in for little visits,
And when you ask them to stay,
They take it seriously.
They never fail to tell you how badly you look;
And they relate little anecdotes
About friends of theirs who went into Declines.
Their conversation consists entirely of Insides;
They are never out of a Critical Condition.
They are always posing for X-ray portraits
Of parts of their anatomy with names like parlor-cars.
They say the doctor tells them
That they have only one chance in a hundred—
The odds aren't big enough.

Then there are In-Laws,
The Necessary Evils of Matrimony.
The only things they don't say about you
Are the ones they can't pronounce.
No matter what you do,
They know a better way to do it.
They are eternally searching your house for dust;
If they can't find any,
It is a wasted day.

They are always getting their feelings hurt
So that they can go around with martyred expressions
And say that you will appreciate them when they're gone—
You certainly will.

There are Nephews;
They are the lowest form of animal life.
They are forever saying bright things
And there is no known force that can keep them
From reciting little pieces about Our Flag.
They have the real Keystone sense of humor—
They are always firing things off in your ear,
Or pulling away the chair you are about to sit on.
Whenever you are striving to impress anyone,
They always appear
And try out the new words they learned from the ice-man—
I wish the Government would draft all males under ten!

And then there are Husbands;
The White Woman's Burden.
They never notice when you wear anything new—
You have to point it out.
They tell you about the deal they put through,
Or the approach they made,
And you are supposed to get all worked up.
They are always hanging around outside your door
And they are incessantly pulling out watches,
And saying, "Aren't you dressed yet?"

They were never known to be wrong;
Everything is always your fault.
And whenever you go out to have a good time,
You always meet them—
I wish to Heaven somebody would alienate their affections.

I hate Relatives;
They cramp my style.

SLACKERS

A HATE SONG

I hate Slackers;
They get on my nerves.

There are the Conscientious Objectors.
They are the real German atrocities.
They go around saying, "War is a terrible thing,"
As if it were an original line.
They take the war as a personal affront;
They didn't start it—and that lets them out.
They point out how much harder it is
To stay at home and take care of their consciences
Than to go and have some good, clean fun in a nice,
    comfortable trench.
They explain that it isn't a matter of mere bravery;
They only wish they had the chance to suffer for their
    convictions—
I hope to God they get their wish!

Then there are the Socialists;
The Professional Bad Sports.
They don't want anybody to have any fun.
If anybody else has more than two dollars,
They consider it a criminal offense.
They look as if the chambermaid forgot to dust them.
There is something about their political views
That makes them wear soiled decolleté shirts,
And they are too full of the spirit of brotherhood
To ask any fellow creature to cut their hair.

They are always telling their troubles to the New Republic;
And are forever blocking the traffic with parades.
If anyone disagrees with them
They immediately go on strike.
They will prove—with a street corner and a soap box—
That the whole darned war was Morgan's fault—
Boy, page an alienist.

There are the Pacifists;
They have chronic stiff necks
From turning the other cheek,
They say they don't believe in war—
As if it were Santa Claus or the Stork.
They will do anything on earth to have peace
Except go out and win it.
Of course they are the only people
Who disapprove of war;
Everybody else thinks it's perfectly great—
The Allies are only fighting
Because it keeps them out in the open air
They know that if we'd all go around wearing lilies,
And simply refusing to fight,
The Kaiser would take his army and go right back home.
It's all wrong, Pershing, it's all wrong.

And then there are the Men of Affairs;
The ones who are too busy to fight.

Business is too good,
And men aren't needed yet, anyway—
Wait till the Germans come over here.
They tell you it would be just their luck
To waste three or four months in a training camp,
And then have peace declared.
It isn't as if they hadn't dependents;
Their wives' relatives can barely buy tires for the Rolls-Royce.
Of course, they may be called in the draft,
But they know they can easily get themselves exempted,
Because they have every symptom of hay fever—
I wish I were head of the draft board!

I hate Slackers;
They get on my nerves.

BOHEMIANS

A HATE SONG

I hate Bohemians;
They shatter my morale.

There are the Artists;
The Inventors of the Nude,
They are always gesticulating with their thumbs,
And sketching, with forks, on table cloths;
They point out all the different colors in a sunset
As if they were trying to sell it to you;
They are forever messing around with batik;
And hanging yellow tassels on things;
And stencilling everything within reach.
I do hope that Gibson never learns what they think of him:
It would simply break his heart.
Of course, they know that being hung in the Academy
Is just a matter of pull.
They say that James Montgomery Flagg may stoop to mere success,
But as for them,
Let them starve first!
Fair enough!

There are the Writers;
The Press Agents for Sex.
They are forever exposing their inmost souls,
Their "stuff" is always "brutally frank"—
Why, they'd just as soon tell you their favorite flower.
They find their fullest expression in free verse;

They call it that
Because they have to give it away.
They are extremely well read,
They can quote from their own works for hours—
Without a mistake.
They are always pulling manuscripts out of their pockets,
And asking you to tell them, honestly—is it too daring?
They would sit down
And write the Great American Novel
If they only could find a publisher Big Enough.
Oh, well—
Genius is an infinite capacity for giving pains.

There are the Actors;
They always refer to themselves as "Players."
Whenever two or three of them are gathered together
Another little theatre comes into the world.
They are eternally leasing vacant kitchenettes
And presenting their own dramas—with Woolworth scenery.
Of course, there can be no real drama above Fourteenth Street.
If they even walked across Times Square
They'd feel that they had lost their amateur standing.
They ask you what you think of their technique,
And then wait for you to commit perjury.
They thank God that they never descended to commercialism;
They know that they'll never be appreciated—
They don't know the half of it.

And then there are the Radicals;
The Table D'Hôte Bolsheviki.
They are always in revolt about something.
Nothing has been done yet that they can wholly approve of.
Their existence is just like Heaven—
There is neither marrying nor giving in marriage.
They are forever starting magazines
And letting the Postal Authorities put the finish to them.
Their one ambition is to get themselves arrested,
So that they can come out and be Heroes.
They are always stifled—
Always longing to loose the trivial fetters of Convention,
And go far away—back to the Real—
I wish they'd get started!

I hate Bohemians;
They shatter my morale.

OH, LOOK—I CAN DO IT, TOO

SHOWING THAT ANYONE CAN WRITE MODERNIST VERSE

BACCHANALE

Hand in hand, we ran through the Autumn forest;
Our laughter soaring on the wings of the mad wind;
In and out, tracing a fantastic path,
Through the passionate, flaming dogwood
And the slim, virginal birches,
Our limbs flashing white against the riotous background.
The grape-leaves I twined rested lightly on your hair,
And, as we ran, you shouted snatches of wild songs—
Pagan hymns of praise to the dead gods.
On we rushed, dizzy with the strong wine of Autumn. . . .
I wonder if you were married, too.

SUNDAY

A litter of newspapers
Piled in smothering profusion.
Supplements sprawling shamelessly open,
Flaunting their lurid contents—
"Divorced Seven Times, Will Re-Wed First Wife,"
Unopened sheets of "help" advertisements;
Editorials, crumpled in a frenzy of ennui;
Society pages, black with lying photographs.
Endless, beginningless heaps of newspapers. . . .
Outside, a thin gray rain,
Falling, falling hopelessly,

With a dull monotony of meaningless sound,
Like the voice of a minister reading the marriage service.

THE PICTURE GALLERY

My life is like a picture gallery,
With narrow aisles wherein the spectators may walk.
The pictures themselves are hung to the best advantage;
So that the good ones draw immediate attention.
Now and then, one is so cleverly hung,
That, though it seems unobtrusive,
It catches the most flattering light.
Even the daubs are shown so skillfully
That the shadows soften them into beauty. . . .
My life is like a picture gallery,
With a few pictures turned discreetly to the wall.

FRAGMENT

We came face to face in the crowd;
Hemmed all about by pushing, straining figures,
Berserk with the thought of getting home to dinner.
Heavy about us rose the odor of crowded humanity,
Hot in our ears sounded their polyglot curses.
But the crowd was kind, for it pushed you into my arms,
There you rested, one supreme moment,
Your delicate body quivering with exquisite timidity.

We stood, we two alone, on the pinnacle of rapture,
Our souls throbbing together.
Then we were torn apart.
But Hope leaped high within me,
For, before you were borne away from me,
You whispered a few shy syllables—
The answer to my feverish question. . . .
Why did you give me the wrong telephone number?

OUR OFFICE

AN INTIMATE GLIMPSE OF VANITY FAIR—EN FAMILLE

A HATE SONG

I hate the Office;
It cuts in on my social life.

There is the Art Department;
The Cover Hounds.
They are always explaining how the photographing machine
    works.
And they stand around in the green light
And look as if they had been found drowned.
They are forever discovering Great Geniuses;
They never fail to find exceptional talents
In any feminine artist under twenty-five.
Whenever the illustrations are late
The fault invariably lies with the editorial department.
They are always rushing around looking for sketches,
And writing mysterious numbers on the backs of photographs,
And cutting out pictures and pasting them into scrapbooks,
And then they say nobody can realize how hard they are
    worked—
They said something.

Then there is the Editorial Department;
The Literary Lights.
They are just a little holier than other people
Because they can write classics about
" 'Brevity is the soul of lingerie,' said this little chemise to
    itself";

242

And "Here are five reasons for the success of the Broadway
    plays."
They are all full of soul;
Someone is forever stepping on their temperaments.
They are constantly having nervous breakdowns
And going away for a few weeks.
And they only come in on Saturday mornings
To hold the franchise.
They tell you what good training editorial work is.
But they don't mean to stay in it—
Some day they will be Free Lances
And write the Great Thoughts that Surge within them.
They say they only wish they could get away from the office—
That makes it unanimous.

Then there is the Fashion Department;
First Aids to Baron de Meyer.
If any garment costs less than $485
They think you ought to give it to the Belgians.
They look at everything you have on,
And then smile tolerantly
And say, "Sears, Roebuck certainly do a wonderful business,
    don't they?"
They are forever taking pictures of prominent Wild Women
Dressed as brides and kneeling at Property Altars.
And they write essays on Smart Fashions for Limited Incomes—
The sky's the limit.

There is the Boss;
The Great White Chief.
He made us what we are to-day—
I hope he's satisfied.
He has some bizarre ideas
About his employees' getting to work
At nine o'clock in the morning—
As if they were a lot of milkmen.
He has never been known to see you
When you arrive at 8:45,
But try to come in at a quarter past ten
And he will always go up in the elevator with you.
He goes to Paris on the slightest provocation
And nobody knows why he has to stay there so long.
Oh, well—
You can't expect to keep him down on the farm.

I hate the Office;
It cuts in on my social life.

ACTORS

A HATE SONG

I hate Actors;
They ruin my evenings.

There are the Juveniles;
The Male Ingenues.
They always interpret the rôles of wealthy young sportsmen,
So that they can come running on in white flannels,
Carrying tennis racquets, and wearing spiked shoes.
Whenever the lights go up
They are discovered with their arms around some girl.
They wear their watches and handkerchiefs on their arms,
And they simply couldn't play a scene without their cigarette cases.
They think that the three Greatest Names in American History
Are Hart, Schaffner, and Marx.
They are constantly giving interviews to the Sunday papers
Complaining about the car-loads of mash notes they receive.
They know they have it in them to do something Really Big;
They relate how Belasco told them that they would go far—
I wish they were on their way!

There are the Movie Heroes;
The Boys Who Drove the Wild West Wild.
They are forever fading out into the sunset,
And if they can't pose for a close-up every few feet
They sue the company.
They wear their hair bobbed,
And always look as if they dressed by mail.

They were never known to lose a fight;
The whole troupe of supernumeraries hasn't a chance against them.
They are just bubbling over with animal spirits—
They are continually walking up the side of houses,
Or springing from one galloping horse to another,
Or leaping out of balloons, without parachutes.
And they love to be photographed balancing on one foot
On the extreme edge of the Grand Canyon—
Oh, that I might get behind them, just once!

Then there are the Tragedians;
The Ones Who Made Shakespeare famous.
They are always telling what they used to say to Booth.
And they talk about the old traditions
As if they had collaborated on them.
They make their positively last appearance semi-annually,
And they are just about to go on farewell tour No. 118397, Series H.
They never appear in any rôle
In which they have to wear long trousers.
If they stooped to play in any drama written after 1700,
They know that Art could never be the same.
They are forever striding around the stage in trick tempests,
Wearing aluminum armor, and waving property swords,
And shrieking at Heaven to do its worst—
I wish Heaven would kindly oblige.

And there are the Drawing-Room Stars;
The Ones That Swing a Mean Tea-Cup.
They always appear in those dramas
In which the Big Line is "No cream, please—lemon."
They interpret every emotion
By tapping the left thumb-nail with the cork-tipped cigarette.
They are invariably the best-dressed men on our stage—
Their press-agent says so himself.
They are always standing in the center of the stage
Saying cutting things about marriage;
And they hang around in property moonlight,
Making middle-aged love.
They cherish secret ambitions
To take off their cutaways and play Hamlet:
They know they could be great
If the public would only give them their just due—
If it only would!

I hate Actors;
They ruin my evenings.

LETTER TO ROBERT BENCHLEY

ROUGHING IT IN THE COUNTRY AT THE BIRCHES, MAINE

Greetings to all from the pine-scented woods!
We hope everybody is feeling so good.
Kindly forgive our writing in pencil;
It's too much trouble to get the other utensil.
We want to tell you about this place.
With us it certainly stands like an ace.
To-day we went out on the lake to fish;
That you were with us, was our heartiest wish.
We caught a trout, not to mention some chubbs,
And then put them back, like a couple of dubs.
A salmon then got on the line by mistake,
But we put him back, for the little ones' sake.
The lake at times is fairly rough.
We go out upon it, though.
The water is cold and full of salmon,
And the scenery hereabouts is charming.
Our Septoline has given out—
We're better off, there's not a doubt.
But still, we'd like a dash of hootch,
In fact, we'd like it very much.
As yet, we have not been in bathing,
We're waiting for a warmer occasion.
We're saving our bathing-suits, crisp and new,
To give to some Ziegfeld ingenue.
The trail around the island's fine;
To-day we saw some porcupines.
The tennis court is a perfect whale;
We thought at first it was part of the trail.

The Wallace Frye just broke a shaft—
You should have heard the captain laugh!
Some children here have the whooping-cough.
If we don't get it, we'll be in soft.
The desk clerk's manner is proud and airy,
Nevertheless, we think he's a fairy.
There are some people right next door
Who turned out to be a terrible bore.
There always seems to be some kind of a hitch
Isn't Nature a (finish this line for yourself, and get a year's
     subscription to the Boston Post.)
The captain's trousers may be out at the seat;
But he stands ace-high with Mr. Bradstreet.
He should worry about cash in hand,
He's got a rating of 800 thous*and*.
Each time the boat sails, he's on her
To collect 54 cents from each passenger.
We expect to be back on Sunday noon,
Or if not then, some fine day soon.
We'll return to the city, 'mid sighs and tears,
With vacation over for another year.
We're feeling fine—the same to you,
And now it's late, we must say adieu.
We think of you all, on the Biltmore roof
And wish you were with us, that's the God's truth.
We watch the flickering firelight,
And wonder if Duggie and Robby are tight.

In the firelight glow, so cheery and warm,
We weep over the mortgage on the Benchley farm.
And now we cannot write any more,
So, once again, we must say au revoir.

OUR OWN HOME TALENT

Miss Isadora Quigley pays
   Terpsichore devotion;
In rhythmic bliss, she bends and sways—
   The true *vers libre* of motion.
She blithely bounds o'er field and stream,
   Attired with Greek simplicity,
And gives, the while, her basic scheme
   A lot of free publicity.
Her genius is, as all agree
   Who watch her do her dances,
An infinite capacity
   For taking awful chances.

You may not care for it—but there!
It keeps her in the open air.

The name of Mr. Eustace Young,
   Our author, sharp and Shavian,
Some day will be on every tongue—
   Including Scandinavian.
He has, he's often told, a *flair*
   For tense and throbbing crudity;
On every page his soul lies bare,
   In literary nudity.
Already he is hailed as great
   By cultural minorities,
For all his works have been, to date,
   Suppressed by the authorities.

Our *literati* have confessed
Nothing succeeds like the suppressed.

Now art Miss Iris Blount employs;
   Her batik and her stencil
Express her maiden griefs and joys,
   She swings a wicked pencil!
In forms of cube and octagon,
   Ignoring technicalities,
She splashes her impressions on,
   In broadest generalities.
She paints no view of moonlit glen,
   No landscape, green and grassy;
Her subjects run to gentlemen
   And ladies, in their chassis.

Her art, our connoisseurs imply,
Is all in the beholder's eye.

To down all kings and presidents
   Our Mr. Tench proposes;
His loudly uttered sentiments
   Are redder than the roses.
He urges anarchism's cause
   In terms concise, but notable;
And what he says about the laws
   Would scarcely pass as quotable.

He pleads that marriages be few,
  While love be free, in plenty—
Which last endears him greatly to
  The local *cognoscenti*.

His word is law, among our set,
On rules of sovietiquette.

BORES

A HYMN OF HATE

I hate Bores;
They take the joy out of my life.

There are the Symptom Collectors.
They have tried every specialist once.
They go about, quoting what they said under ether;
They give readings from their fever-charts;
And they carry their cast-off appendixes with them, in bottles—
Just for old times' sake.
They are forever showing you X-ray photographs
Of their quaint crannies and intimate inglenooks.
They say that you can never guess what they suffer,
And then they clear up all doubts.
Every doctor tells them that their case is hopeless—
I'll say it is.

Then there are the Parlor Comedians.
They have memorized the entire series
Of history's favorite anecdotes.
They begin by saying that they just heard a new one—
Which is the funniest line in the whole story.
They go in strongly for the kind of humor
That requires special apparatus.
They will go miles to procure an exploding cigar
Or a perforated drinking-glass.
They have a repertoire of sure-fire comedy hits:
They address all waiters as "George."

And they love to call you on the telephone
And say, "This is Police Headquarters speaking."
They save up all their witticisms for you,
And tell you how everyone nearly dies at them—
Nearly dies is right.

There are the Gluttons for Business.
They started on a shoe string
And worked their way up to white spats.
They are entirely self-made,
And think that everybody is clamoring for the recipe.
Their life is an open ledger;
They tell you all the inside gossip
About invoices and bills of lading,
And illustrate their talk with diagrams
Showing their increased output throughout the Middle West.
They relate heart-rending stories
Of how they haven't had a vacation in ten years,
And how they wish they could go away for a while—
And I wish they could go away from now on.

And there are the Amateur Mediums.
They are always fooling around with the spirits.
They are constantly receiving messages from the Great Beyond
Saying Uncle Walter is well
And hopes everybody at home is the same.
They spend every night
Being warned, in dreams, of their friends' deaths.
There is nothing that they can't worm out of a ouija board.

They are so messy around the house;
They are always tipping tables
And sitting around in circles, with the lights out.
They are forever seeing things and hearing knocks,
And they just know they have clairvoyant minds—
If any.

I hate Bores;
They take the joy out of my life.

WITH BEST WISHES

Glad Christmas Day once more has come—
　　There's little novelty in that.
It's welcomed eagerly by some,
　　Which isn't to be marveled at.
Their stockings hold a house and lot
　　(I hope you gather what I mean),
A picturesquely furnished yacht.
　　A next year's model limousine,
A sable wrap of graceful cut,
　　A sheaf of cheques for vast amounts;
It's not the thought that matters, but
　　The gift which goes with it that counts.

But I'LL get a multitude of seasonable cards,
　　A bowl full of lily bulbs, approaching their decease;
A pair of gilded shoe-trees, with appropriate regards,
　　And a leather-bound "Evangeline," with colored frontispiece.

It's scarcely any wonder that
　　The season finds me all unmoved,
For Father Christmas leaves me flat—
　　Step-Father Christmas, it has proved.
'Twas ever thus—from early youth
　　I've seen my hopes decay, because
Too soon I learned the bitter truth:
　　There isn't any Santa Claus.
Each Yuletide mocks my touching trust;
　　The give and let give is my plea,
It's Christmas Day for some, but just
　　December twenty-fifth for me.

For I'LL *get a paper-weight, to crush my Christmas cheer,*
  A hand-painted needle-case, a brace of button-hooks,
A host of cordial wishes for a prosperous new year,
  And a holiday edition of the "Rubaiyat," de luxe.

I've often heard that some there are—
  How hard such tales are to believe!
To prove that costlier by far
  It is to give than to receive.
On Christmas they present their friends
  With motor cars, and pearls in strings,
And blocks of stock with dividends,
  And other useful little things.
Though I have no such benefits,
  I sing the Christmas spirit's praise.
I know the giver's thrill—for it's
  A poor Yule which won't work both ways.

So I'LL *give a laundry bag, of chintz refined, yet gay;*
  A tooth-brush container of a fanciful design,
A flock of timely greetings for a snappy Christmas Day,
  And a highly colored copy of "That Old Sweetheart of Mine."

INVICTUS

Farthest am I from perfection's heights,
   Faulty am I as I well could be,
Still I insist on my share of rights.
   When I am dead, think this of me:
Though I have uttered the words "Yea, bo,"
   Though I use "ain't" to get a laugh,
Though I am wont to explain "Let's go,"
   Though I say "You don't know the half"—
Black through my record as darkest jet,
   Give me, I beg, my devil's due;
Only remember, I've never yet
   Said, "How's the world been treating you?"

"What could be sweeter?" I fondly muse;
   "You said a mouthful," I confess;
Witnesses testify that I use
   "Yes, indeedy," in times of stress;
"Oh, it's a great life," I loudly claim—
   "If you don't weaken," I amend;
"I'll tell the world," is my middle name;
   "Well, how's the boy?" I greet a friend.
While I acknowledge each grave defect,
   Still I am master of my fate—
All that I ask you is, Recollect
   I never said, "I'm here to state."

"Yours till hell freezes," I sign my mail;
  "I'll say it is," I coyly cry;
"What's the good word?" is my cheery hail;
  Bidding farewell, I say "Bye-bye";
I demand, "How do you get that way?"
  "Oh, have a heart," is all my plea;
Speaking of oysters, I sadly say,
  "I like them, but they don't like me."

Humbly I own to each one of these,
  Yet I alone for all my slips;
Heap me a measure of credit, please—
  "Kiddie" has never passed my lips.

SONG OF THE OPEN COUNTRY

When lights are low, and the day has died,
I sit and dream of the countryside.

Where sky meets earth at the meadow's end,
  I dream of a clean and wind-swept space
Where each tall tree is a stanch old friend,
  And each frail bud turns a trusting face.
A purling brook, with each purl a pray'r,
  To the bending grass its secret tells;
While, softly borne on the scented air,
  Comes the far-off chime of chapel bells.
A tiny cottage I seem to see,
  In its quaint old garden set apart;
And a Sabbath calm steals over me,
  While peace dwells deep in my brooding heart.

And I thank whatever gods look down
That I am living right here in town.

THE PASSIONATE FREUDIAN TO HIS LOVE

Only name the day, and we'll fly away
    In the face of old traditions,
To a sheltered spot, by the world forgot,
    Where we'll park our inhibitions.
Come and gaze in eyes where the lovelight lies
    As it psychoanalyzes,
And when once you glean what your fantasies mean
    Life will hold no more surprises.
When you've told your love what you're thinking of
    Things will be much more informal;
Through a sunlit land we'll go hand-in-hand,
    Drifting gently back to normal.

While the pale moon gleams, we will dream sweet dreams,
    And I'll win your admiration,
For it's only fair to admit I'm there
    With a mean interpretation.
In the sunrise glow we will whisper low
    Of the scenes our dreams have painted,
And when you're advised what they symbolized
    We'll begin to feel acquainted.
So we'll gaily float in a slumber boat
    Where subconscious waves dash wildly;
In the stars' soft light, we will say good-night—
    And "good-night!" will put it mildly.

Our desires shall be from repressions free—
    As it's only right to treat them.
To your ego's whims I will sing sweet hymns,

    And *ad libido* repeat them.
With your hand in mine, idly we'll recline
    Amid bowers of neuroses,
While the sun seeks rest in the great red west
    We will sit and match psychoses.
So come dwell a while on that distant isle
    In the brilliant tropic weather;
Where a Freud in need is a Freud indeed,
    We'll be always Jung together.

THE DRAMA

A HYMN OF HATE

I hate the Drama;
It cuts in on my sleep.

There is the Clean Play;
The one you take Aunt Etta to see
After a day's sightseeing in the financial district.
The hero is the man from Back Home,
With the blameless life and the creaseless trousers—
A real rough rhinestone.
He may not be so strong on grammar,
But he loves children and sleeping outdoors.
The heroine sneers at him in Act I,
But after he has shown up the effete aristocracy,
And received news that they've struck oil
Back in the Little Marigold well,
She listens to reason.
And when the curtain falls at eleven o'clock,
They are starting out for the Great, Clean West together—
Three hours too late.

Then there is the Comedy of Manners;
The manners provide most of the comedy.
It is all about the goings-on in titled circles—
How Her Grace's handkerchief
Was found in Sir Arthur's diggings.
Tea flows like water,
Butlers are everywhere,

And there is practically no stint to the epigrams
About there being two kinds of husbands:
Your own, and the kind that is in love with you.
Everybody stands about,
Gesticulating with cucumber sandwiches,
And saying, "Oh, Lord Cyril, what a cynic you are!"
There is always a little country ingenue
Who tearfully goes back home in the last act,
Declaring that those society people are all rotten—
She said it.

There is the Farthest North performance
Of the Play That Makes You Think—
Makes you think that you should have gone to the movies.
It is translated from the Norwegian;
They might just as well give it in the original.
All the lighting is dim
So that the actors' faces can scarcely be distinguished,
Which is doubtless all for the best.
The heroine is invariably Misunderstood—
Probably because of her accent.
She is a regular little Glad Girl,
Always falling in love with an innocent bystander,
Or finding that she has married her uncle by mistake,
Or going out into the night and slamming the door.
And things come to a rousing climax
In a nice, restful suicide, or a promising case of insanity.
You tell 'em, Ibsen; you've got the Scandinavian rights.

And there is the Allegorical Drama;
It becomes as sounding brass or a tinkling symbol.
The critics can always find subtle shades of meaning in it—
The triumph of mind over Maeterlinck.
The actors play the parts
Of Light, Joy, Beauty, and Imagination,
While the audience represent Ennui and Bewilderment.
The leading character is searching for Happiness.
And after hunting through four acts, twenty-seven scenes,
And a company of three hundred, exclusive of stage-hands,
He finally discovers it at home—
Would to Heaven he had looked there in the first place!

I hate the Drama;
It cuts in on my sleep.

PARTIES

A HYMN OF HATE

I hate Parties;
They bring out the worst in me.

There is the Novelty Affair,
Given by the woman
Who is awfully clever at that sort of thing.
Everybody must come in fancy dress;
There are always eleven Old-Fashioned Girls,
And fourteen Hawaiian gentlemen
Wearing the native costume
Of last season's tennis clothes, with a wreath around the neck.

The hostess introduces a series of clean, home games:
Each participant is given a fair chance
To guess the number of seeds in a cucumber,
Or thread a needle against time,
Or see how many names of wild flowers he knows.
Ice cream in trick formations,
And punch like Volstead used to make
Buoy up the players after the mental strain.
You have to tell the hostess that it's a riot,
And she says she'll just die if you don't come to her next party—
If only a guarantee went with that!

Then there is the Bridge Festival.
The winner is awarded an arts-and-crafts hearth-brush,
And all the rest get garlands of hothouse raspberries.

You cut for partners
And draw the man who wrote the game.
He won't let bygones be bygones;
After each hand
He starts getting personal about your motives in leading clubs,
And one word frequently leads to another.

At the next table
You have one of those partners
Who says it is nothing but a game, after all.
He trumps your ace
And tries to laugh it off.
And yet they shoot men like Elwell.

There is the Day in the Country;
It seems more like a week.
All the contestants are wedged into automobiles,
And you are allotted the space between two ladies
Who close in on you.
The party gets a nice early start,
Because everybody wants to make a long day of it—
They get their wish.
Everyone contributes a basket of lunch;
Each person has it all figured out
That no one else will think of bringing hard-boiled eggs.

There is intensive picking of dogwood,
And no one is quite sure what poison ivy is like;

They find out by the next day.
Things start off with a rush.
Everybody joins in the old songs,
And points out cloud effects,
And puts in a good word for the color of the grass.

But after the first fifty miles,
Nature doesn't go over so big,
And singing belongs to the lost arts.
There is a slight spurt on the homestretch,
And everyone exclaims over how beautiful the lights of the city look—
I'll say they do.

And there is the informal little Dinner Party;
The lowest form of taking nourishment.
The man on your left draws diagrams with a fork,
Illustrating the way he is going to have the new sun-parlor built on;
And the one on your right
Explains how soon business conditions will be better, and why.

When the more material part of the evening is over,
You have your choice of listening to the Harry Lauder records,
Or having the hostess hem you in
And show you the snapshots of the baby they took last summer.

Just before you break away,
You mutter something to the host and hostess
About sometime soon you must have them over—
Over your dead body.

I hate Parties;
They bring out the worst in me.

LOVE SONG

Suppose we two were cast away
    On some deserted strand,
Where in the breeze the palm trees sway—
    A sunlit wonderland;
Where never human footstep fell,
    Where tropic love-birds woo,
Like Eve and Adam we could dwell,
    In paradise, for two.
Would you, I wonder, tire of me
    As sunny days went by,
And would you welcome joyously
    A steamer? . . . So would I.

Suppose we sought bucolic ways
    And led the simple life,
Away—as runs the happy phrase—
    From cities' toil and strife.
There you and I could live alone,
    And share our hopes and fears.
A small-town Darby and his Joan,
    We'd face the quiet years.
I wonder, would you ever learn
    My charms could pall on you,
And would you let your fancy turn
    To others? . . . I would, too.

Between us two (suppose once more)
    Had rolled the bounding deep;
You journeyed to a foreign shore,
    And left me here to weep.
I wonder if you'd be the same,
    Though we were far apart,
And if you'd always bear my name
    Engraved upon your heart.
Or would you bask in other smiles,
    And, charmed by novelty,
Forget the one so many miles
    Away? . . . That goes for me.

IDYL

Think of the things that can never come true—
  Save in the shadowy country of dreams.
Think of what might be, for me and for you,
  Could we but shatter the world's sorry schemes.
Think of our own little vine-covered nest;
  Each day, at sunset, I'd wait for you there,
Down by the gate, in the glow of the west,
  Dressed all in white, with a rose in my hair.

Think of a chair, softly-cushioned and wide;
  Think of a hearth, where the red firelight dies;
Think of me sitting there, close by your side,
  Reading the stories writ deep in your eyes.
Think of the years, like an unending song,
  Think of a quiet we never have known.
While, all forgotten, the world rolls along,
  Think of us two, in a world of our own.

Now that you've thought of it seriously—
Isn't it great that it never can be?

MOVIES

A HYMN OF HATE

I hate Movies;
They lower my vitality.

There is the Great Spectacle.
Its press-agent admits
That it is the most remarkable picture ever made.
The story is taken from history,
But the scenario writer smoothes things over a little,
And makes Cleopatra Antony's wife,
Or has Salome marry John the Baptist,
So that you can bring the kiddies.
The management compiles vital statistics
About the size of the cast:
How the entire population of California
Takes part in the battle scenes;
And where the beads worn by the star would reach
If placed end to end.
The audience sits panting
And says, "Think of what it must have cost to produce it!"
Think what could have been saved by not producing it!

Then there is the Picture with Sex Appeal;
The appeal is still unanswered.
The production goes to show
That bad taste, off the screen,
Is still in its infancy.
It seeks to reveal the depths to which society has fallen,
And it proves its point.

It gives glimpses of Night Life in the Great City:
The revelers are shown wearing fancy paper hats,
And marching in lockstep around the table,
And shamelessly performing the two-step.
The characters are always driving home in motors
To the Public Library, or Senator Clark's house.
The interiors are designed
By the man who decorates dentists' waiting-rooms.
The star is a prominent vampire
Who is a nice, sweet girl when she is at home,
And supports an indulgent husband
In the style to which he has become accustomed;
The wages of sin is $3,500 a week.

There is the High Art Production:
They charge three dollars a seat for it—
That's where they get the "high."
The photography is always tricky;
The actors seem to be enveloped in a dense fog,
And that goes for the plot, too.
There is some idea of an allegorical strain running through it,
So that, whenever things are beginning to get good,
And the heroine is just about to fall,
The scene changes
To a panorama of storm clouds,
Or a still-life study of apple blossoms,
Or a view of Hong-Kong harbor by moonlight.

Every few minutes, there is a close-up of the star
Registering one of her three expressions.
The sub-titles offer positive proof
That there is a place where bad metaphors go when they die.
The critics agree unanimously
That the picture removes all doubt
As to whether movies should be classed among the arts—
Removes all doubt is right.

And there is the News of the Week.
It is assembled on the principle
That no news is good news.
It shows all the big events in current history:
The paperweight manufacturers' convention in Des Moines;
The procession of floats during Anti-Litter Week in Topeka;
And the sailors of the U.S.S. Mississippi
Grouped to form the words "E Pluribus Unum."
There is always a view of a wrecked schooner,
Enabling the pianist to oblige with "Asleep in the Deep."
When they have a chance to show a picture of a fire
They color it a mean shade of red.
Before you can get a good look at the event before you,
The scene changes to a new one
Leaving the fate of the people in the last picture hanging—
It's too good for them.

I hate Movies;
They lower my vitality.

TO MY DOG

I often wonder why on earth
    You rate yourself so highly;
A shameless parasite, from birth
    You've lived the life of Reilly.
No claims to fame distinguish you;
    Your talents are not many;
You're constantly unfaithful to
    Your better self—if any.
Yet you believe, with faith profound,
    The world revolves around you;
May I point out, it staggered 'round
    For centuries without you?

In beauty, you're convinced you lead,
    While others only follow.
You think you look like Wallace Reid,
    Or, at the least, Apollo.
The fatal charms with which you're blest,
    You fancy, spell perfection;
The notion, may I not suggest,
    Is open to correction?
An alien streak your tail betrays;
    Your ears aren't what they would be;
Your mother was—forgive the phrase—
    No better than she should be.

One can but feel your gaiety
    Is somewhat over-hearty;
You take it on yourself to be

The life of every party.
In bearing, while no doubt sincere,
   You're frankly too informal.
And mentally, I sometimes fear,
   You're slightly under normal.
The least attention turns your brain,
   Repressions slip their tether;
Pray spare your friends the nervous strain
   And pull yourself together!

You take no thought for others' good
   In all your daily dealings,
I ask you, as a mother would,
   Where *are* your finer feelings?
I think I've seldom run across
   A life so far from lawful;
Your manners are a total loss,
   Your morals, something awful.
Perhaps you'll ask, as many do,
   What I endure your thrall for?
'Twas ever thus—it's such as you
   That women always fall for.

ABSENCE

I never thought that heav'n would lose its blue
   And sullen storm-clouds mask the gentle sky;
I never thought the rose's velvet hue
   Would pale and sicken, though we said good-by.
I never dreamed the lark would hush its note
   As day succeeded ever-drearier day,
Nor knew the song that swelled the robin's throat
   Would fade to silence, when you went away.

I never knew the sun's irradiant beams
   Upon the brooding earth no more would shine,
Nor thought that only in my mocking dreams
   Would happiness that once I knew be mine.
I never thought the slim moon, mournfully,
   Would shroud her pallid self in murky night.
Dear heart, I never thought these things would be—
   I never thought they would, and I was right.

LYRIC

How the arrogant iris would wither and fade
    If the soft summer dew never fell.
And the timid arbutus that hides in the shade
    Would no longer make fragrant the dell!
All the silver-flecked fishes would languish and die
    Were it not for the foam-spangled streams;
Little brooks could not flow, without rain from the sky;
    Nor a poet get on without dreams.

If the blossoms refused their pale honey, the bees
    Must in idleness hunger and pine;
While the moss cannot live, when it's torn from the trees,
    Nor the waxen-globed mistletoe twine.
Were it not for the sunshine, the birds wouldn't sing,
    And the heavens would never be blue.
But of all Nature's works, the most wonderful thing
    Is how well I get on without you.

SONG FOR THE FIRST OF THE MONTH

Money cannot fill our needs,
   Bags of gold have little worth:
Thoughtful ways and kindly deeds
   Make a heaven here on earth.
Riches do not always score,
   Loving words are better far.
Just one helpful act is more
   Than a gaudy motor car.
Happy thoughts contentment bring
   Crabbed millionaires can't know;
Money doesn't mean a thing—
   Try to tell the butcher so!

None can stretch his life an hour
   Though he offer boundless wealth:
Money, spite of all its pow'r,
   Cannot purchase ruddy health.
Simple pleasures are the best,
   Riches bring but misery,
Homely hearts are happiest,
   Joy laughs loud at poverty.
Pity those in Mammon's thrall,
   Poor, misguided souls are they,
Money's nothing, after all—
   Make the grocer think that way!

Greatest minds the world has known
   All agree that gold is dross
Man can't live by wealth alone;
   Bank books are a total loss.
Banish strife and greed and gloom,
   Throw off money's harsh control,
Sow good deeds, and watch them bloom—
   Hyacinths, to feed the soul.
Hoard no pelf, lest moth and rust
   Do their work and leave you flat.
Money? It is less than dust—
   Laugh the landlord off with that!

FULFILMENT

I do not sit and sigh for wealth untold,
   It never thrusts itself into my schemes;
I shrink from all your piles of clanking gold—
   Better my sparkling hoard of golden dreams.
A life of limousined and jeweled ease
   Is but a round of fathomless *ennui.*
Your motor cars, your pearls, your sables—these
   Are naught to me.

Better a homely flat in Harlem's wilds
   Than a costly living's spurious benefits;
Better a simple butter-cake at Childs'
   Than caviar and stalled ox at the Ritz.
Your unearned gold, to me, is shot with flaws;
   A life of honest toil I'd make my lot—
Which really makes it very nice, because
   It's what I've got.

LYNN FONTANNE

Dulcy, take our gratitude,
   All your words are golden ones.
Mistress of the platitude,
   Queen of all the old ones.
You, at last, are something new
   'Neath the theatre's dome. I'd
Mention to the cosmos, you
   Swing a wicked bromide.

Heroines we've known, to date,
   Scattered scintillations
(Courtesy the Wilde estate)
   Through their conversations.
Polished line and sparkling jest—
   They've provided plenty.
Dulcy's bromides brought us rest—
   Dulcy far niente.

TO MARJORIE RAMBEAU

IN "DADDY'S GONE A-HUNTING"

If all the tears you shed so lavishly
   Were gathered, as they left each brimming eye.
And were collected in a crystal sea,
   The envious ocean would curl up and dry—
So awful in its mightiness, that lake,
   So fathomless, that clear and salty deep.
For, oh, it seems your gentle heart must break,
   To see you weep.

We try to tell ourselves it isn't true,
   We strive to feel that dawn must follow dark,
We strain to hold the thought that, off-stage, you
   Are happy as the widely-mentioned lark.
But, though you wring our feelings to their cores,
   Our devastated hearts you seem to keep,
For, oh, we pack the theatre to its doors
   To see you weep.

CHRISTMAS, 1921

I do not ask you for presents rare,
   Other-world trove of forgotten metals;
Orchids that opened to jungle air,
   Tropical hate in their writhing petals;
Onyx and ebony, black as pain,
   Carved with a patience beyond believing;
Perfumes, to harry the startled brain;
   Laces that women have died in weaving;
Cool-tinted pearls from the ocean, where
   Grottoes of dolorous green regret them.
I do not ask you for presents rare—
   Dearest, I know that I wouldn't get them.

Give me your love, on this Christmas Day.
   Give me your thoughts, when the chimes are ringing.
Send me the happier along my way,
   Deep in my soul let your words be singing.
Give me your wishes, as bells sound clear,
   Charming the air with their golden measure.
Give me your hopes for the unborn year,
   Fill up my heart with a secret treasure.
Give me the things that you long to say,
   All of your tenderest dreams unfetter.
Give me your love, on this Christmas Day—
   But come across, please, when times get better.

MARILYN MILLER

From the alley's gloom and chill
   Up to fame danced *Sally*.
Which was nice for her, but still
   Rough upon the alley.
How it must regret her wiles.
   All her ways and glances.
Now the theatre owns her smiles,
   Sallies, songs, and dances.

Ever onward *Sally* goes—
   Life's one thing that's certain.
O'er the end of other shows
   Let us draw a curtain.
Their untimely ends are sad,
   But they stood no chances,
For, you see, they never had
   Sally's songs and dances.

BOOKS

I hate Books;
They tire my eyes.

There is the Account of Happy Days in Far Tahiti;
The booklet of South Sea Island resorts.
After his four weeks in the South Seas,
The author's English gets pretty rusty
And he has to keep dropping into the native dialect.
He implies that his greatest hardship
Was fighting off the advances of the local girls,
But the rest of the book
Was probably founded on fact.
You can pick up a lot of handy information
On how to serve *poi,*
And where the legend of the breadfruit tree got its start,
And how to take *kava* or let it alone
The author says it's the only life
And as good as promises
That sometime he is going to throw over his writing,
And go end his days with Laughing Sea-pig, the half-caste
    Knockout—
Why wait?

Then there is the Little Book of Whimsical Essays;
Not a headache in a libraryful.
The author comes right out and tells his favorite foods,
And how much he likes his pipe,
And what his walking-stick means to him—
A thrill on every page.
The essays clean up all doubt
On what the author feels when riding in the subway,

288

Or strolling along the Palisades.
The writer seems to be going ahead on the idea
That it isn't such a bad old world, after all;
He drowses along
Under the influence of Pollyanesthetics.
No one is ever known to buy the book;
You find it on the guest room night-table,
Or win it at a Five Hundred Party,
Or someone gives it to you for Easter
And follows that up by asking you how you liked it—
Say it with raspberries!

There is the novel of Primitive Emotions;
The Last Word in Unbridled Passions—
Last but not leashed.
The author writes about sex
As if he were the boy who got up the idea.
The hero and heroine may be running wild in the Sahara,
Or camping informally on a desert island,
Or just knocking around the city,
But the plot is always the same—
They never quite make the grade.
The man turns out to be the son of a nobleman,
Or the woman the world's greatest heiress,
And they marry and go to live together—
That can't hold much novelty for them.
It is but a question of time till the book is made into a movie,
Which is no blow to its writer.

People laugh it off
By admitting that it may not be the highest form of art;
But then, they plead, the author must live—
What's the big idea?

And then there is the Realistic Novel;
Five hundred pages without a snicker.
It is practically an open secret
That the book is two dollars' worth of the author's own
    experiences,
And that if he had not been through them,
It would never have been written,
Which would have been all right with me.
It presents a picture of quiet family life—
Of how little Rosemary yearns to knife Grandpa,
And Father wishes Mother were cold in her grave,
And Bobby wants to marry his big brother.
The author's idea of action
Is to make one of his characters spill the cereal.
The big scene of the book
Is the heroine's decision to make over her old taffeta.
All the characters are in a bad way;
They have a lot of trouble with their suppressions.
The author is constantly explaining that they are all being
    stifled—
I wish to God he'd give them the air!

I hate Books;
They tire my eyes.

FRAGMENT

Why should we set these hearts of ours above
    The rest, and cramp them in possession's clutch?
Poor things, we gasp and strain to capture love,
    And in our hands, it powders at our touch.
We turn the fragrant pages of the past,
    Mournful with scent of passion's faded flow'rs,
On every one we read, "Love cannot last"—
    So how could ours?

It is the quest that thrills, and not the gain,
    The mad pursuit, and not the cornering:
Love caught is but a drop of April rain,
    But bloom upon the moth's translucent wing.
Why should you dare to hope that you and I
    Could make love's fitful flash a lasting flame?
Still, if you think it's only fair to try—
    Well, I am game.

FIGURES IN POPULAR LITERATURE

THE SHEIK

The desert chieftain here behold,
   The Dempsey of the Nile.
He knocks the lady readers cold
   And cramps their husbands' style.
The heroine reels back for more.
   They play like happy kids—
He tells his love, then knocks her for
   A row of pyramids.

She revels in his gallant deeds;
   Her passions higher mount
Each time he languidly proceeds
   To drop her for the count.
They marry in the end—they do
   In all such compositions—
And now, no doubt, he'll knock her through
   Another twelve editions.

So if you'd knock the ladies dead,
Just use your right and go ahead.

THE FLAPPER

The playful flapper here we see,
   The fairest of the fair.
She's not what Grandma used to be—
   You might say, *au contraire.*

Her girlish ways may make a stir,
　　Her manners cause a scene,
But there is no more harm in her
　　Than in a submarine.

She nightly knocks for many a goal
　　The usual dancing men.
Her speed is great, but her control
　　Is something else again.
All spotlights focus on her pranks,
　　All tongues her prowess herald,
For which she may well tender thanks
　　To God and Scott Fitzgerald.

Her golden rule is plain enough—
Just get them young and treat them rough.

CHANTEY

A wet sheet and a straining sail,
   And a sea of shifting blue;
A wide sky and a rousing gale,
   And joy in the heart of you;
A clean line, where the sky hangs low
   And a seagull soars and dips;
And the old voice that bids men go—
   Go down to the sea in ships.

So go and sail the gold sea, the bold sea, the cold sea;
The waving, craving, raving sea that's fringed with silken foam;
Oh, go and sail the green sea, the keen sea, the mean sea—
But if it's all the same to you, I'll stick around at home.

The swift turn of the night-wind's whim,
   And the tang of hempen strings;
The sharp snap of the halyards slim,
   And the spray that cuts and stings.
The wild chorus the breezes hum,
   And the waves that prowl and creep;
And the old voice that bids men come—
   Come over the tameless deep.

So go and sail the white sea, the light sea, the bright sea,
The dashing, crashing, smashing sea, that dances in the gale;
Go on and sail the sad sea, the bad sea, the mad sea—
But if it's just the same to you, I'd rather be in jail.

Maude, the brightest of the sex,
Forged her daddy's name to checks,
Took them to the local banks,
Cashed them, with a smile of thanks.
All the money came in handy—
Maudie was so fond of candy!
Weight she gained in way affrighting,
So she's given up her writing.

Save the money, when you forge;
Little ladies do not gorge.

Don, the little apple-cheek,
Sold his aunt's blue-ribbon Peke,
Sneaked it out of Auntie's house,
Hidden in his sailor blouse.
Donald planned to spend his earnings
Gratifying all his yearnings.
But the chance for pleasure slipped him,
For the doggie's buyer gypped him.

If they can't complete the deal,
Nicer children do not steal.

LIFE'S VALENTINES

PRINCESS MARY AND VISCOUNT LASCELLES

Here behold, and likewise lo,
Princess Mary and her beau.
Bright her cheek with maiden blush;
Shall we say a royal flush?
How we've watched their love's ascents
In the Sunday supplements!
Blessings for the happy pair;
For their photographs—the air!

MR. DAVID WARK GRIFFITH

Look, and you will surely find
Right above, the Master Mind.
(Just a nickname of his own
Which he worked up all alone.)
He it was who made, they say,
Movies what they are to-day;
This the goal for which he's tried—
Lord, I hope he's satisfied!

DAVID BELASCO

Often in the local press
On your kindness you lay stress.
Love's the basis of your art,
So you say—that is, in part.
Frequently you tell us of
How devotedly you love

Actors, public, critics, too . . .
Echo answers, "Yes, you do."

CALVIN COOLIDGE

"Ah," we said; and eke "At last.
Things won't be as in the past;
Once vice-presidents were nil,
But our Fighting Calvin will
All such precedents destroy."
"Ah," we said; and "Atta boy!". . .
Now we wonder dolefully
What's become of Calvin C.?

DR. FRANK CRANE

Daily you distribute praise
'Mong clean books and wholesome plays.
Honest toil and hard-earned gold,
Kindness to the weak and old;
Where would all the virtues be
Without such publicity?
Wealth untold you're paid, per line,
Won't you be my Valentine?

AVERY HOPWOOD

How you must have loved, when small,
Chalking words upon a wall!

"Ladies' Night" we owe to you,
"Getting Gertie's Garter," too.
Gaily gath'ring royalties
On your bedroom phantasies,
Ever heavier grows your purse
As you go from bed to worse.

FLORENZ ZIEGFELD

Still we're groggy from the blow
Dealt us—by the famous Flo;
After 1924,
He announces, nevermore
Will his shows our senses greet—
At a cost of five per seat.
Hasten, Time, your onward drive—
Welcome, 1925!

JOHN WANAMAKER

On the advertising page
Scintillates our dry good sage.
Not a text that Honest John
Cannot write a sermon on.
Readers live from day to day
Just to see what he will say.
"Have you seen his last?" they cry.
"Would to God I had," says I.

THE FAR-SIGHTED MUSE

Dark though the clouds, they are silver-lined;
  (This is the stuff that they like to read.)
If Winter comes, Spring is right behind;
  (This is the stuff that the people need.)
Smile, and the World will smile back at you;
  Aim with a grin, and you cannot miss;
Laugh off your woes, and you won't feel blue.
  (Poetry pays when it's done like this.)

Whatever it is, is completely sweet;
  (This is the stuff that will bring in gold.)
Just to be living's a perfect treat;
  (This is the stuff that will knock them cold.)
How could we, any of us, be sad?
  Always our blessings outweighing our ills;
Always there's something to make us glad.
  (This is the way you can pay your bills.)

Everything's great, in this good old world;
  (This is the stuff they can always use.)
God's in His heaven, the hill's dew-pearled;
  (This will provide for the baby's shoes.)
Hunger and War, do not mean a thing;
  Everything's rosy, where'er we roam;
Hark, how the little birds gaily sing!
  (This is what fetches the bacon home.)

FIGURES IN POPULAR LITERATURE

THE DRAB HEROINE

There was a time, as doubtless you're
   Enabled to recall,
When heroines of literature
   Were not like this at all.
Their hair was heaped in glinting curls,
   Their forms were wondrous fair,
And when it came to sex, the girls
   Admittedly were there.

To-day, toward woolen lingerie
   The lady's thoughts are turned,
And sex is in its infancy
   So far as she's concerned.

A kitchen drudge, whom all ignore,
   She leads a life entrancing
As Cinderella's was, before
   She took up ballroom dancing.

Abandon hope, and learn to cook,
And you will figure in a book.

PAGING SAINT PATRICK

The good Saint Patrick, in his day,
   Performed a worthy act:
He up and drove the snakes away,
   With more technique than tact.
Could he descend from realms above
   And roam about New York,
He'd find it reminiscent of
   The good old days in Cork.
The snakes he knew could never tie
   The brand our village has—
The kind that daily multiply
   And thrive on tea and jazz.

Should he his tales of snakes relate
   We'd strive to hide a laugh;
For, though the saint was wise and great,
   He didn't know the half.
Where'er he'd go, to dine or dance,
   Or lunch, or tea, or sup,
The saint would have a splendid chance
   To do some cleaning up.
Could he but leave his present star,
   He'd see that things were changed—
How sad such little visits are
   Not easily arranged!

MOOD

Unless I yield my love to you, you swear
   In strangely distant countries must you dwell;
Denied this heart of mine, you could not bear
   These dear, familiar scenes we've loved so well.
To-morrows that will come, you could not face
   With only pain to bear you company,
Among the whispering memories of this place,
   The little, intimate things that speak of me.

Where mighty mountains rear their cruel height,
   The world between us, would you dwell, apart;
Where curious peace, that comes with tropic night,
   Answers the bitter question of your heart.
The lilac bush, that bends with bloom in May,
   The winding path, the arbor where we sat.
These things should know you nevermore, you say—
   Ah, love, if I could only count on that!

TRIOLETS

Herewith I send you my heart,
   Marking it "Fragile—don't break it."
Rather a radical start—
Herewith I send you my heart;
Take it, I beg, in good part
   (That is, assuming you'll take it).
Herewith I send you my heart,
   Marking it "Fragile—don't break it."

Take me, or let me alone—
   What, after all, does it matter?
Ever my feelings you've known;
Take it, or let me alone—
Though, I might readily own,
   I'd recommend you the latter.
Take me, or let me alone—
   What, after all, does it matter?

Sweet, I have waited too long;
   Heedless and wanton I've tarried.
Silenced forever my song—
Sweet, I have waited too long.
Bitter the hemlock, and strong—
   Now you have gone and got married!
Sweet, I have waited too long;
   Heedless and wanton, I've tarried.

FIGURES IN POPULAR LITERATURE

THE WESTERN HERO

This hero ranks among the best—
    He's Nature's rugged child.
You've heard about the woolly West?
    'Twas he who drove it wild.
Observe that he is dressed to kill
    (Forgive the pun, I pray),
In pranks like this he finds a thrill—
    He's simply full of play.

In his revolver terrors lurk;
    His aim's a deadly one.
Could Annie Oakley see his work,
    She'd throw away her gun.
He trifles not with woman's love,
    In spite of his virility,
For he's a charter member of
    The natural nobility.

He shoots to kill and aims to please;
Our books are filled with such as these.

THE YOUNGER SET

A HYMN OF HATE

I hate the Younger Set;
They harden my arteries.

There are the Boy Authors;
The ones who are going to put *belles lettres* on their feet.
Every night before they go to sleep
They kneel down and ask H. L. Mencken
To bless them and make them good boys.
They are always carrying volumes with home-cut pages,
And saying that after all, there is only one Remy de Gourmont;
Which doesn't get any dissension out of me.
They shrink from publicity
As you or I would
From the gift of a million dollars.
At the drop of a hat
They will give readings from their works—
In department stores,
Or grain elevators,
Or ladies' dressing-rooms.
It is pretty hard to get them to show you their work;
Sometimes you even have to ask them to.
They are constantly backing you into corners,
And asking you to glance over some little things
That they just dashed off in a spare year—
Read 'em and weep!

Then there are the Male Flappers;
The Usual Dancing Men.

They can drink one straight Orange Pekoe after another,
And you'd never know that they had had a thing.
Four débutante parties a night is bogie for them,
And their talk is very small indeed.
They never claimed to go so big at a desk,
But they can balance a plate of chicken salad, a cup of bouillon,
And a guest-room-size napkin,
And make gestures with the other hand.
They are mean boys when the orchestra starts;
They work in so many wise steps
That you can't tell whether it's a waltz or a track-meet.
No one can tie them, at a charity entertainment;
They say they have often been told
That with their talent
And the way they can wear clothes
They are simply wasting time on the amateur stage—
I can't give them any argument on that one.

There are the Black Sheep;
The Boys with the Nasty Records.
They are always giving you glimpses of the darker side of life—
Telling you what time they got to bed yesterday morning
And how many people passed out cold,
And where they went from there.
They virtually admit
That if they ever turned over a new leaf
The bootlegging industry would go straight to smash.
They are so inured to alcohol,

That as soon as they've had one cocktail,
They want to go right out and address the Senate.
They are always consulting little red notebooks,
Containing names, telephone numbers, and authors' notes,
And it is an open secret that they have met an actress.
They tell you they know they are going the pace that kills,
And then they laugh bitterly,
And say, "But what does it matter?"—
They took the words right out of my mouth.

And there are the Heavy Thinkers;
The Gluttons for Head-Work.
They have got up a lot of novel ideas
About everybody having a right to live his own life,
And about marriage being just a few words
Muttered over you by a minister.
They say that there may be
Some Supreme Force back of the universe;
They will look into that when they get the time.
Just stand back and give them room,
And they will drop the conventions for the count.
They are pretty low in their minds about America;
They hint that its civilization
Is practically plucking at the coverlet,
And that the Other Side is the only place for intellectuals—
Bon voyage!

I hate the Younger Set;
They harden my arteries.

TO MYRTILLA, ON EASTER DAY

Myrtilla's tripping down the street,
   In Easter finery.
The Easter blooms are not more sweet
   And radiant-hued than she.
The rarest woodland violets were
   Less fragrant than her frills,
The sunny-tinted hair of her
   Would shame the daffodils.
Ah, many a heart-beat halts and skips,
   And sighs pursue her way,
As down the street Myrtilla trips,
   This joyous Easter Day.

Myrtilla's tripping gaily by,
   In Easter garb arrayed.
Ah, would the lads as deeply sigh
   For any other maid?
The lads, they come from far and near,
   When down the street she starts;
Oh, lightly step, Myrtilla dear,
   Your path is strewn with hearts.
The maids are held in envy's grips,
   For they are left, forlorn,
As down the street Myrtilla trips,
   This glorious Easter morn.

Ah, well may echo, sweet as love,
     Her laugh's delicious lilt,
For sure she knows the power of
     Her Easter bonnet's tilt;
A master wrought, with tender care,
     Each dainty frill and flounce;
The fragrance of her, cool and rare,
     Costs thirty-five per ounce.
Parisian rouge defines her lips,
     And pearls her throat bedeck—
As down the street Myrtilla trips,
     I hope she breaks her neck!

FIGURES IN POPULAR LITERATURE

THE GLAD GIRL

This child of curious tendencies
    To your acquaintance add.
Her smile is permanent, for she's
    The gladdest of the glad.
Come battle, famine, flood, or fire,
    The cheery little one
Accepts it as her heart's desire,
    And says, "Ain't we got fun?"

The joy of living fills her cup;
    Of hope, she's never rid.
Imagine how she'd brighten up
    Your household—God forbid!
The bitter ills her fortunes send
    She sprinkles smiles galore on;
It seems to me our little friend
    Is something of a moron.

But if I had her author's pelf,
I'm sure that I'd be glad, myself.

THE BOY SAVANT

Behold, in all his native state,
    Dispensing truths profound,
The gifted undergraduate,
    The learned campus hound.

His reading fills his youthful head
   With thoughts that throb and hum,
For Nietzsche, as is often said,
   Abhors a vacuum.

In lighter moments, he's the man
   That fills the flappers' dreams;
He'd make the All-American—
If there were petting teams.
His self-regard is scarcely small,
   His conversation shows it;
Just ask him anything at all—
   For he's the boy that knows it.

Oh, youth verbose, our feelings spare—
For God, for country, and forbear!

Little Gormley stole a purse.
Took it from his crippled nurse.
It was quite a lucky touch—
She'd been saving for a crutch.
So our hero, for a starter,
Bought a seat for "Gertie's Garter."
Spent in vain his gains unlawful—
For he thought the show was awful!

When *you* plunder Nursie's hoard.
Spend it where you won't be bored.

Gracie, with her golden curls,
Took her mother's string of pearls.
Figuring—as who would not?
It would pawn for quite a lot.
Picture, then, her indignation
When she found it imitation!
Though her grief she tries to smother,
Grace can't feel the same towards Mother!

All pretence and sham detest;
Work for nothing but the best.

Earnest—such a little man!
Got his family's sedan.
Drove it over hill and dale—
Just escaped the county jail—

Maimed, in his exhilaration,
Folk of spotless reputation.
But his trip with gloom was tainted—
Now the car must be repainted!

Strive to keep the death-rate low—
Think how high repair bills go!

POEM IN THE AMERICAN MANNER

I dunno yer highfalutin' words, but here's th' way it seems
When I'm peekin' out th' winder o' my little House o Dreams;
I've been lookin' 'roun' this big ol' world, as bizzy as a hive,
An' I want t' tell ye, neighbor mine, it's good t' be alive.
I've ben settin' here, a-thinkin' hard, an' say, it seems t' me
That this big ol' world is jest about as good as it kin be,
With its starvin' little babies, an' its battles, an' its strikes,
An' its profiteers, an' hold-up men—th' dawggone little tykes!
An' its hungry men that fought fer us, that nobody employs.
An' I think, "Why, shucks, we're jest a lot o' grown-up little
    boys!"
An' I settle back, an' light my pipe, an' reach fer Mother's hand,
An' I wouldn't swap my peace o' mind fer nothin' in the land;
Fer this world uv ours, that jest was made fer folks like me an'
    you
Is a purty good ol' place t' live—say, neighbor, ain't it true?

THOUGHTS

Yes, my love, I think about you
   In the morning's roseate flush;
Heavy hang the clouds, without you,
   Sullen seems the dawning's blush.
In the slender, graceful grasses,
   Silver-tipped with sparkling dew,
In the woodland's shadowy masses
   All that I can see is you.

When the noon-day sun is burning,
   Hot the scented air, and clear,
Then to you my thoughts are turning,
   And I would that you were here.
Then I dream that, happy vagrants,
   We are wandering hand in hand
Through the lanes of light and fragrance
   Into Summer's fairyland.

When the weary sun is sinking,
   And the blossoms close, in rest,
Then of you, my love, I'm thinking,
   As I watch the brilliant west.
When the little stars show faintly
   In the Maxfield Parrish sky,
When the moon gleams, cold and saintly,
   Then to you my fancies fly.

When the frightened owls are calling,
   And the sombre midnight reigns,
Thick and fast the shades come crawling,
   Like the thoughts of fevered brains,
When life trembles at the brink of
   Death's unfathomable deep,
You're the last thing that I think of—
   Goodness knows, I need some sleep.

FANTASY

Did we love each other, sweetest,
  Skies would be forever blue;
Time would flutter by on fleetest
  Wings of glittering golden hue.
Joy beyond a poet's telling
  Should we learn the meaning of;
Arcady would be our dwelling—
  Did we love.

Did we love each other, darling,
  Banished ugliness and gloom;
Ever sweet would pipe the starling,
  Ever gay the rose would bloom.
Care and trouble could not find us,
  Bliss untold would be our lot.
But, one scarcely need remind us,
  We do not.

MEN I'M NOT MARRIED TO

No matter where my route may lie,
   No matter whither I repair,
In brief—no matter how or why
   Or when I go, the boys are there.
On lane and byway, street and square,
   On alley, path and avenue,
They seem to spring up everywhere—
   The men I am not married to.

I watch them as they pass me by;
   At each in wonderment I stare,
And "But for heaven's grace," I cry,
   "There goes the guy whose name I'd bear!"
They represent no species rare,
   They walk and talk as others do;
They're fair to see—but only fair—
   The men I am not married to.

I'm sure that to a mother's eye
   Is each potentially a bear;
But though at home they rank ace-high,
   No change of heart could I declare.
Yet worry silvers not their hair;
   They deck them not with sprigs of rue.
It's curious how they do not care—
   The men I am not married to.

L'Envoi

In fact, if they'd a chance to share
  Their lot with me, a lifetime through,
They'd doubtless tender me the air—
  The men I am not married to.

WOODLAND SONG

The hothouses' offerings, costly and rare,
    Cannot ape the forget-me-not's blue;
Blooms forced to perfection can't hope to compare
    With the lowly anemone's hue.
The humble wild rose, unassuming and meek,
    Must have stolen the setting sun's glow;
The blushes which play o'er its delicate cheek
    Are of tints that no palette may know.

No matter how lovely these flowers may be,
Gardenias and orchids look better to me.

The purple-eyed violet, fragrantly cool,
    Spends its beauty extravagantly.
The waxen-white lily that sleeps on the pool
    Gives its loveliness lavishly free.
Their glorious petals the poppies unfold
    For whoever may happen to pass,
And Nature, made mad by the buttercups' gold,
    Flings it wantonly over the grass.

But my favorite blossoms, I'm here to aver,
Are American Beauties at five dollars per.

RONDEAU [1]

It isn't fair, to me, when you're away.
In vain the clouds their brightest hues display.
   Sweet Summer dons in vain her gladdest guise—
   The vision falls but coldly on my eyes;
The sky seems draped in melancholy gray.

Though never bloomed the roses half so gay,
Though never half so radiant shone the day,
   This loveliness my stubborn heart denies;
      It isn't fair.

And do you, also, sing a minor lay?
Do you to bitter yearnings fall a prey?
   "Well, no," frank Echo honestly replies,
   "In fact, it is distinctly otherwise."
And that, my dear, is why again I say
      It isn't fair.

FIGURES IN POPULAR LITERATURE

THE GREAT LOVER

I'm sure you've met this lad before;
  His work is fast, though rough.
He feels that all is fair in war—
  In love, it's fair enough.
His tale the Vice-Suppressor takes,
  And drinks in every word
(A single swallow never makes
  A Sumner, we have heard).

Our hero lived in ages gone—
  The days of bright romance.
We read about his goings-on
  And sigh, "So this is France!"
You must concede, the boy was good
  Among the local ladies;
But his intentions toward them would
  Not pave the streets of Hades.

How sweet to read of days of old
When knights, to say the least, were bold!

ROSEMARY [1]

Ah, no, I dare not lose myself in dreams
    Of that dead day we ne'er shall know again;
So pitifully brief a while it seems,
    So sharp the thought of you, as you were then.
The poignant memories of little things—
    A flower in your coat, a frock I wore;
The wistful autumns, and the troubling springs—
    I dare not let them come to me once more.

The tender gloamings, when we two would stray
    Where locusts hung their frothy blooms above;
The violets—like my eyes, you used to say;
    The rustic bridge, where first you spoke of love;
The words we whispered, while the summer breeze
    Fluttered the grasses with its scented breath;
Ah, no, I dare not summon thoughts like these;
    I'm so afraid I'd laugh myself to death.

SONG [1]

And shall we build a little nest
   In Arcady, in Arcady,
Where we can settle down and rest
   In sweet security;
A place where sunbeams cast their spell,
   And shadows play, and shadows play,
Where you and I and Love can dwell
   Forever and a day?

And shall we go there, you and I,
   In poppy time, in poppy time,
When fluffy cloudlets dot the sky
   And clustered roses climb?
And shall we watch the seasons wane,
   And come and go, and come and go,
And welcome April's golden rain,
   And hail December's snow?

And will no other ever find
   Our garden spot, our garden spot?
And shall we leave the world behind
   And count it well forgot?
There boundless peace can come to us,
   But trouble can't, but trouble can't.
And shall we live forever thus?
   You bet your life we shan't.

SUMMER RESORTS

A HYMN OF HATE

I hate Summer Resorts;
They ruin my vacation.

There is the Seaside Hotel.
The booklets say that it is right on the water,
And they aren't much over quarter-of-a-mile out of the way.
You are never at a loss for something to do;
You can go down by the waves
And watch the gentleman in sneakers
Trying out his Little Admiral water-wings,
Or you can sit on the porch
And listen to the lady in the next rocker
Explain that this is the first Summer she has ever been to a place
Where the rates were less than fifteen dollars a day.
There is always lots of excitement down on the beach—
Group photographs are constantly being taken.
And posses are being formed to find the person or persons
Who took the garters out of bathhouse number 38
And if you play your cards right,
You may be able to find a dead horseshoe crab.
The more highly-strung guests take you aside and tell you
How much the water means to them.
And how they wish they could stay there beside it for ever and
    ever—
Good here!

And there is the place where you can get Back to Nature,
Or even farther.
The house was built
When electric lights were regarded as Edison's Folly,
And the surface of plumbing has only been scratched,

And the proprietor hasn't got around to making any changes.
You can tell the tennis court by the net:
Otherwise you would think it was an old-fashioned rock garden
Planted with all the flowers mentioned in Shakespeare's works,
And if you want to play golf,
You will find a course three counties to the left.
The guests are like one big family—
Just like that.
You sit at the table with a lady from Montclair
Who gives talks on the trouble that Junior has had with his
   tonsils.
Everyone says how restful it all is,
And how it seems as if the city must be a thousand miles away—
It's an under-estimate.

There is the Synthetic Newport;
Luke-warm Dog!
The life is pretty fairly speedy;
Many of the young married set inhale right out in public.
Silver frequently changes hands after the bridge games.
And you'd almost think the cocktails were made of the real
   stuff—
That goes for the whole works.
Extra-mural affection is generally indulged in:
If you sit down next to your own husband,
It's all over the country club that you are insanely jealous of him.
The revelers have their intellectual side, too;
There is scarcely one of them that hasn't read "The Sheik,"

They are the first to concede that they are hitting things up.
They say that there won't be a thing left of them
If they keep up the pace all Summer—
Stay with 'em, boys!

And then there is the Mountain Resort;
The Home of American Scenery.
You can go yodling up Old Baldy—
Five hundred feet above sea level—
Or you can collect postcard views of Lovers' Leap,
To pass around among your friends on Winter evenings.
You can't conscientiously call it a Summer
Until you get a good, clear day
When you can figure out Washington's profile in the peaks—
You can see a better one on a two-cent stamp
Even when it's raining.
The gossip on the porch keeps you right on the edge of your seat;
One transient tells how he is pretty sure he saw a trout jump,
And hardly has the uproar died down
Before someone else claims to have found some genuine
        maidenhair fern.
The guests are seldom without a kind word for the landscape,
And they have nothing but praise to offer the air—
It's all theirs.

I hate Summer Resorts;
They ruin my vacation.

GRANDFATHER SAID IT

When I was but a little thing of two, or maybe three,
My granddad—on my mother's side—would lift me on his
    knee;
He'd take my thumb from out my mouth and say to me: "My
    dear,
Remember what I tell you when you're choosing a career:

    "Take in laundry work; cart off dust;
    Drive a moving van if you must;
    Shovel off the pavement when the snow lies white;
    But think of your family, and please don't write."

When I was two I cannot say his counsel knocked me cold.
But now it all returns—for, darling, I am growing old,
And when I read the writing of the authors of today
I echo all those golden words that grandpa used to say:

    "Clean out ferryboats; peddle fish;
    Go be chorus men if you wish;
    Rob your neighbors' houses in the dark midnight;
    But think of your families, and please don't write."

MONODY

Slowly the roses droop and die;
  (Where is the love we knew of old?)
Slowly the sun-bright days go by.
  (Little white love, so cold, so cold.)
Dark are the leaves on the weary ground,
  Sad are the winds in the still, gray glen;
Slowly the year goes its listless round
  Over again.

Somewhere the sunbeams dance and play;
  (Where is the love that used to thrill?)
Somewhere the riotous roses sway,
  (Little white love, so still, so still.)
Somewhere the skies of young April shine
  Bright as the heavens we prayed to then . . .
Somewhere you're pulling the same old line
  Over again.

SOMEWHAT DELAYED SPRING SONG

Crocuses are springing,
Birds are lightly winging,
Corydon is singing
  To his rustic lute;
Sullen winter passes,
Shepherds meet their lasses,
Tender-tinted grasses
  Shoot.

All the world's a-thrilling,
Meadow larks are shrilling,
Little brooks are trilling,
  You, alone, are mute;
Why do you delay it?
Love's a game—let's play it,
Go ahead and say it—
  Shoot!

SONNET [1]

Sweeter your laugh than trill of lark at dawn.
   As marble richly gleams, so shines your throat.
The grace of you would shame the pale young fawn;
   Rather than walk, like silken down you float.
Lighter your touch than fall of April rain;
   Cooler your cheek than petal washed with dew.
Whene'er you speak, all gladness and all pain
   Speak also, in the throbbing voice of you.

Like blossom on its stem is poised your head,
   Wrapped closely round about with fragrant bands.
As roses' passionate hearts, your mouth is red;
   Like lilies in the wind, your long white hands.
Brighter the glance of you than summer star;
   But, lady fair, how awful thick you are!

TO A LADY

Lady, pretty lady, delicate and sweet,
    Timorous as April, frolicsome as May,
Many are the hearts that lie beneath your feet
    As they go a-dancing down the sunlit way.

Lady, pretty lady, blithe as trilling birds,
    Shy as early sunbeams play your sudden smile.
How you quaintly prattle lilting baby words,
    Fluttering your helpless little hands the while!

Lady, pretty lady, bright your eyes and blue,
    Who could be a-counting all the hearts they broke?
Not a man you meet that doesn't fall for you;
    Lady, pretty lady, how I hope you choke!

MEMORIES

Once, you say, we felt love's blisses
    When the world was not so wise;
Once, you say, you knew my kisses
    Under Babylonian skies.
There fulfilled our scorching passion,
    There we pledged our tender vow—
Strange we meet in this cold fashion
    Here and now.

Maybe you were, as you've stated,
    Fooling round in Babylon;
Maybe you participated
    In the local goings-on.
Maybe things like that befell you,
    Ages past. But anyhow,
I was never there, I'll tell you
    Here and now.

PROMISE

Love beyond my maddest dreaming
   You have sworn you'll show to me;
You will guide me to the gleaming,
   Reeling heights of ecstasy.
Dizzier joy than else could reach me,
   Fiercer bliss and wilder thrill,
All of this some day you'll teach me,
   Y-e-e-s you will!

RONDEAU [2]

Give me a rose, cool-petaled, virgin white,
Pure as the morning, mystical as night;
   Not bold gardenias, flaunting their expense
   Like courtesans, in perfumed insolence,
Nor brazen orchids, feverishly bright.

Give me no hothouse violets, cold, polite,
With lengths of costly ribbon girdled tight—
   Matrons, in corseted magnificence;
            Give me a rose.

One girlish blossom proffer as your mite.
Ah, lovelier by far within my sight
   Than rich exotics' glamorous pretense
   Is one shy rose, sweet in its diffidence.
And then besides, my love, the price is right;
            Give me a rose.

SONG OF THE CONVENTIONS

We'd dance, with grapes in our wind-tossed hair,
    And garments of swirling smoke;
We'd fling wild song to the amorous air,
    Till the long-dead gods awoke.
Our quivering bodies, young and white,
    Poised light by the brooklet's brink,
We'd whirl and leap through the moon-mad night—
    But what would the neighbors think?

We'd bid the workaday world go hang,
    And idle the seasons through;
We'd pay no tribute of thought or pang
    To the world that once we knew.
With hearts in ecstasy intertwined,
    In languorous, sweet content,
We'd leave all worry and care behind—
    But how would we pay the rent?

We'd roam the universe, hand in hand,
    Through tropical climes, or cold,
And find each spot was a wonderland,
    A country of pearl and gold.
Our hearts as light as the sunlit foam,
    We'd voyage the oceans o'er,
With never a thought for those at home—
    But wouldn't our folks be sore?

SONG [2]

Clarabelle has golden hair,
   Mabel's eyes are blue,
Nancy's form is passing fair,
   Mary's heart is true.
Chloë's heart has proved to be
   Something else again;
Not so much on looks is she
   But she gets the men.

Doris deals in verse and prose,
   Stella's brow is high,
Martha, swift and skillful, sews,
   Maud can bake a pie.
Chloë neither sews nor cooks,
   Cannot swing a pen,
Doesn't seem to run to books;
   She just gets the men.

Winnie's gayly dancing feet
   Fly on fairy wings;
Silver bells ring, clear and sweet,
   When Belinda sings.
Fair and true and talented
   Are they all—but then
Little Chloë knocks them dead;
   Chloë gets the men.

BALLADE OF UNDERSTANDABLE AMBITIONS

Fame and honor and high degree,
   Jeweled scepter and throne-room plot—
Yellow primroses, they, to me;
   Milder longings are mine, God wot.
Smooth and simple, I'd have my lot;
   I'd depart on another tack.
At my aim give me just one shot—
   All I want is a lot of jack.

Fond communion with field and tree,
   Bread and cheese in an ivied cot;
Sweet and clean though the thought may be,
   I subscribe to it ne'er a jot.
Other yearnings my heart make hot,
   Other cravings my spirit rack.
In my dreams to my goal I trot—
   All I want is a lot of jack.

On the pages of history
   Ne'er my name shall I sign and blot;
I'll go down to posterity
   Neither scholar nor patriot.
Cloaks of Shelley and Keats and Scott
   Ne'er will fall on my humble back;
Immortality ask I not—
   All I want is a lot of jack.

L'Envoi

Prince, or Rover, or Rex, or Spot,
    Ere I die let me take a crack
At the wish which I've never got—
    All I want is a lot of jack.

"HOW BOLD IT IS"

How bold it is, this fine young love we bear;
A high, white flame, to cut the ghostly night;
A virgin armor, burnished hard and bright
To turn the blows of age and death and care!
Too brave a thing it is, to see it break
Beneath the unending taps of little things—
Of sharpened words, and hurried answerings,
And fretful illness, and recited ache,
And tiny jealousies, and whimpering woe,
And household plannings, year on futile year,
And patient "Yes, my love," and "Yes, my dear,"
And "Why did you do thus, and why do so?"

Quick, let us part, that ever our love may be
As now we know it, young and bold and free.

SONG OF A CONTENTED HEART

All sullen blares the wintry blast;
  Beneath gray waves the waters sleep.
Thick are the dizzying flakes and fast;
  The edged air cuts cruel deep.
The stricken trees gaunt limbs extend
  Like whining beggars, shrill with woe;
The cynic heavens do but send,
  In bitter answer, darts of snow.
Stark lies the earth, in misery,
  Beneath grim winter's dreaded spell—
But I have you, and you have me,
  So what the hell, love, what the hell!

The wolf, he crouches at the sill,
  And, grinning, bares expectant fangs,
While heavy o'er the house, and chill,
  The coming of the landlord hangs.
Each moment, on the shrinking door,
  May sound his knocking's hideous din.
And more and more, and ever more,
  The eager bills come trooping in.
The milkman clamors for his due,
  The grocer and the cook, as well—
But you have me, and I have you,
  So what the hell, love, what the hell!

SONG OF THE WILDERNESS

We'll go out to the open spaces,
    Break the web of the morning mist,
Feel the wind on our upflung faces.
    [This, of course, is if you insist.]
We'll go out in the golden season,
    Brave-eyed, gaze at the sun o'erhead.
[Can't you listen, my love, to reason?
    Don't you know that my nose gets red?]
Where the water falls, always louder,
    Deep we'll dive, in the chuckling foam.
[I'll go big without rouge and powder!
    Why on earth don't you leave me home?]

We'll go out where the winds are playing,
    Roam the ways of the brilliant West.
[I was never designed for straying;
    In a taxi I'm at my best.]
Minds blown clean of the thoughts that rankle,
    Far we'll stray where the grasses swirl.
[I'll be certain to turn my ankle;
    Can't you dig up another girl?]
We'll go out where the light comes falling—
    Bars of amber and rose and green.
[Go, my love, if the West is calling!
    Leave me home with a magazine!]

TRIOLET [1]

Give back the heart that I gave;
  Keeping it never can mend it.
See, I can smile, and be brave.
Give back the heart that I gave,
Hold it no more as your slave—
  I've got a new place to send it.
Give back the heart that I gave;
  Keeping it never can mend it.

WANDERLUST

I want to go out to the woodlands green,
    And stand 'neath the mighty trees.
I'm longing to hark to the mournful keen—
    The voice of the wistful breeze.
I'll find me the place where the fox-gloves start,
    And violets coyly bloom,
Where the whispering cypress stands apart
    In mystical, fragrant gloom.
I'll go where the feathery grasses lean
    To gaze in the placid brook;
I want to go out to the woodlands green,
    And never give them a look.

I want to go down to the open sea;
    I'll search for a sunlit strand
Where clean-scented winds blow cool and free
    O'er glittering, swirling sand.
I want to go out on the sparkling shore
    Where frolicsome wavelets play;
I'm yearning to feel on my cheek, once more,
    The kiss of the ardent spray.
There's longing, down deep in the heart of me,
    To look on the sun-shot foam.
I want to go down to the open sea—
    And then I'll come right back home.

I want to go back to a country town,
  Afar from the city's thrills—
A dear little village that's snuggled down
  Asleep, by the guardian hills.
I'm going to stand in the ancient square
  And look to the crimson west
When pealing of chimes, on the quiet air,
  Bids villagers go to rest.
I'm yearning to dress in a gingham gown
  And play with a frisking calf.
I want to go back to a country town,
  And give it a hearty laugh.

A TRIOLET

You'll be returning, one day.
   (Such premonitions are true ones.)
Treading the dew-spangled way,
You'll be returning, one day.
I'll have a few things to say—
   I've learned a whole lot of new ones.
You'll be returning, one day.
    (Such premonitions are true ones.)

WIVES

A HYMN OF HATE

I hate Wives;
Too many people have them.

There are the Splendid Housekeepers;
The Girls Who Shake a Mean Furnace.
Give them a darning-egg, and a box of assorted hooks and eyes,
And they wouldn't change places with Lady Mountbatten.
They keep you right on the edge of your chair
With stories about the stoppage in the kitchen drain,
And how impudent Delia was about those new aprons,
And how they have every reason to believe
That the laundress is taking soap home to her folks.
For comedy relief
They relate how they wise-cracked the butcher
When he told them veal cutlets had gone up.
Their books are their best friends;
They love to browse in "Thirty Pretty Ways to Cook Cauliflower"
Or "Two Hundred Daring Stitches in Filet Crochet."
They can't see why people should want to go out nights;
Their idea of whooping things up
Is to sit by the sewing-table, and listen for Junior's croup.
They are always making second-hand puddings,
Or seeing whether the blue vase doesn't look better on the piano
Than it did on the bookcase.
Oh, well—
It keeps them out of the open air.

Then there are the Veteran Sirens;
The Ones Who Are Wedded, but What of It?
They can take their husbands, or let them alone—
But not in the order named.
Any unmarried man above the age of Jackie Coogan
They regard as All Theirs.
They are constantly helping to fix up bachelor apartments,
Or visiting the male sick, with jars of beef tea,
Or picking out oddities in neckwear for their Boy Friends.
If any man they know goes and gets married,
They feel that they have grounds for a breach of promise suit.
They are always talking in low voices over the telephone,
And carefully dropping letters out of their hand-bags,
And going around full of smiling mystery
About where they are having tea.
They say they wish to goodness
They could have a moment to themselves;
They'd give anything if some nice girl would come along
And take some of their admirers off their hands—
Try and get them!

There are the Drooping Lilies;
The Girls Who Could Have Married That Man with All That Money.
They are always parking a secret sorrow,
And you must guess what the unshed tears are all about.
Their husbands may look normal in public,
But they are Little Better than Animals in the home.
You have no idea what they have to put up with—
Their husbands dance with Another Woman

Twice in the same evening,
Or won't read anything but the newspapers,
Or simply refuse to touch spinach in any form.
If they could only bring themselves
To write down what they have been through
It would be the biggest day that Literature ever saw.
Everyone tells them they might have gone on the stage
And become the toast of the town,
Or put the movies on a paying basis,
Or sent the interior decorating business for a loop—
And here they are—yoked to a lot of Clods!
Things may look pretty black for them now,
But some day,
Some day they know that they will get their due—
I hope to God they will!

And then there are the Regular Little Pals;
More Like Friends than Wives.
They go everywhere with their husbands
Just to hold the franchise.
You find them up at the Polo Grounds
Asking which is the Yankee eleven;
Or on the golf links
Making a fifth in a Sunday morning foursome;
Or lending a feminine touch to a poker game—
Going ahead on the idea that a straight is better than a flush.
They are a big help in their husbands' business affairs;
They are always dropping in at the office
For little surprise visits.

They smile happily at you
And ask you what their husbands would ever do without them—
I'll give you three guesses!

I hate Wives;
Too many people have them.

PAEAN

The sun shines fair, the sun shines true,
    The sun shines golden bright;
The sky takes on a lovelier blue,
    The clouds a daintier white.
The birds trill out a roundelay,
    The rosebuds dance with glee,
Each living thing holds holiday;
    The world belongs to me!

My heart beats loud, my heart beats strong,
    My heart beats fast and high;
Within my soul's a rousing song,
    A light within my eye.
Go, raise the banners high in air,
    And spread the tidings round!
Let drums and trumpets boom and blare,
    For I have lost a pound!

SONG [3]

When summer used to linger,
   Before the daisies died,
You'd but to bend your finger
   And I was by your side.
And, oh, my heart was breaking,
   And, oh, my life was through;
You had me for the taking;
   "Now run along," said you.

But now the summer's over,
   The birds have flown away,
And all the amorous clover
   Has turned to sober hay.
And you're the one to tarry,
   And you're the one to sigh,
And beg me, will I marry.
   "The deuce I will," say I.

AND OBLIGE

When I've made a million dollars—it may take a year or two
    At the present rate of speed that things are going—
There are various little matters that are somewhat overdue,
    And the prospect, at the moment, isn't glowing;
But as soon as I've a million, as I started in to say,
    Life will be, I take it, gloriously happy;
For already I am planning to expend it in a way
    That will be, if I may say it, rather snappy.

I will charter me a taxicab of cheery white and brown,
    And you'll never catch me glancing at the meter!
And I'll make a little tour of all the milliners in town;
    And the question is, Could anything be sweeter?
Just for stamps and lunch and cigarettes, each morn I'll draw a check
    For a thousand dollars, payable to bearer,
And you'll hear the pearls a-clanking, as I drape them on my neck.
    It occurs to me that little could be fairer.

It is true that a million doesn't take you very far,
    And it's hard to find another when you've shot it;
But I'll blow it like the widely known inebriated tar,
    For I want to be a good one while I've got it.
So the minute I've a million, I'll go right ahead and spend,
    Though it doesn't last me more than over Sunday.
'n the meantime, though, I wonder, as a favor to a friend,
    Could you let me have a dollar—say, till Monday?

TRIOLET [2]

It is never the cost of the gift;
   It is the thought that I treasure.
Such affections as mine do not shift.
It is never the cost of the gift—
Which is quite an incentive to thrift;
   Business must come before pleasure.
It is never the cost of the gift;
   It is the thought that I treasure.

BALLADE OF A NOT INSUPPORTABLE LOSS

Who will slacken the mental strain,
   Who'll sit down and explain to me.
This, the riddle that racks my brain,
   This, the theme of my monody?
   I'm a glutton for mystery—
Plots and puzzles to me are clear;
   Just one thing has me up a tree—
Where did the flappers disappear?

What's become of that mighty train.
   All so carefully bold and free.
Each like each, as were drops of rain.
   Short of garment, and frank of knee?
   Do they flap in eternity?
All I know is, they are not here;
   To the riddle, I hold no key—
Where did the flappers disappear?

Think not, reader, that I'd complain.
   Squander on me no sympathy.
Though they've vanished, I feel no pain—
   I get on—rather swimmingly.
   I'd not cavil at Fate's decree;
Rather, give it a rousing cheer,
   Still, there's something I cannot see—
Where did the flappers disappear?

L'Envoi
Prince, you've labored incredibly
  Tracing the snows of yesteryear;
Answer this one, and let that be—
  Where did the flappers disappear?

HUSBANDS

A HYMN OF HATE

I hate Husbands;
They narrow my scope.

There are the Home Bodies;
The Boys for Whom the Marriage Idea Was Got Up.
If it wasn't for them
The suburbs would have shut down long ago.
Give them a hammer and a mouthful of tacks,
And you'll never have to worry about where they spend their
    evenings.
Their business cuts in horribly on their night life:
They can hardly wait to rush back to the love nest
And do their stuff.
Some big undertaking is always on their minds—
If it isn't bobbing the hedge,
It's putting up the new shelf for the preserves.
They take you off into corners,
And tell you the latest good one that's going the rounds
About how much they saved by chopping the kindling wood
    themselves.
They are seldom mistaken for Rudolph Valentino;
The militia has not yet been called out to keep the women back.
They dress right up to their rôle;
The neckties launder without a scruple,
The collars were designed when Gramercy Square was considered
    up-town,
And the suits were tailored by the visiting seamstress.
It isn't as if they never burned up the White Lights;

Every wedding anniversary
They shoot the works
And take the wife to dinner at Ye Golden Glow Waffle Shoppe.
They are always trying to sell matrimony to the old school
    friends.
Their big contention is
That there's nothing like it—
Where's the argument?

Then there are the He-Men;
The Masters in Their Own Homes.
The news about the equality of the sexes
Hasn't got around to them yet.
Their conception of the perfect woman
Is one who sews the buttons on before they come off.
They wouldn't give Helen of Troy a second look
If they heard she wasn't so snappy at darning socks.
They are the life of the household;
If the eggs are done longer than three minutes,
They don't speak until the next month.
If the helpmate is ten minutes late getting home
She has to show a letter from her pastor.
They are great boys on a party;
Any time any one else asks the wife to dance,
They want to plead the Unwritten Law.
Their notion of feminine repartee
Is "Yes, dear, of course you're right."
They say that if things ever got to the point
Where they were not the acknowledged Head of the House,

They would never show their faces again—
That's an idea, too.

There are the Steppers-Out;
Married, but What's That between Friends?
They tell you that the wife is a great little woman,
And that closes the subject.
They show you how tall Junior is with one hand,
And try to guess your weight with the other.
Their conquests are a dark secret;
They don't tell a soul until after they have been introduced
They are always looking for new talent;
Can they help it if the rumor got out
That all the last year's Follies Girls
Are so many withered violets to them?
They may always be found on dance floors
Tiring out the flappers;
Or in dark corners
Telling fortunes by palmistry;
Or leaning up against tea tables,
Crazed with cinnamon toast.
Try to tell them what devils they are,
And all the thanks you get for it
Is their lifelong friendship.
They may be a bit gay,
But there is no more harm in them
Than there is in Mussolini.
They explain that some temperaments can stand restraint,
But as for them,

Give them liberty or give them death—
I wish to God they'd leave the decision with me!

And then there are the Gloom Kings;
The Gluttons for Sympathy.
They are the human Einstein theories—
Nobody at home understands them.
They have a rough time getting their stuff across;
The wife may be all very well in her way,
But when it comes to Understanding,
She can't make the grade.
If only they had married some rising young mind-reader,
They could have saved themselves a lot of trouble.
They wear cynical little smiles,
And go around giving impersonations of Disillusionment.
They tell you that of course they can never say anything,
But sometimes they almost think you know—
Which is a big estimate.
You can see that they wish the wife all the luck in the world
By the way they relate the plans for what they would do
If they were ever free.
They like to toy with the idea
That they will just drop quietly Out of Things some day;
They laugh bitterly,
And say everybody would be better off if they did—
The ayes have it!

I hate Husbands;
They narrow my scope.

SONG OF A HOPEFUL HEART

Oh, time of our lyrical laughter,
  Oh, pageant of glittering days,
The glamourous Aprils—and after,
  The delicate, mystical Mays!
So gallant and sudden and heedless,
  So gayly defiant of regret,
We smiled as we thought how 'twas needless
  To vow that we'd never forget
Those galloping days of our blisses,
  Alike, and yet never the same—
But you have forgotten my kisses,
  And I have forgotten your name.

Oh, always there's one who remembers,
  Who brightens, with memories' glow,
The ponderous, sullen Novembers,
  The colorless Winters, and slow.
Why linger in shadowy sadness?
  Why drape us in lavender hue?
The red of that magical madness
  Our hearts could be wearing anew.
It's only the coward who misses
  The glorious rush of the game—
Try hard to remember my kisses;
  I guess I can think of your name.

SONG [4]

When all the world was younger.
   When petals lay as snow.
What recked I of the hunger
   An empty heart can know?
For love was young and cheery,
   And love was quick and free;
To-morrow might be weary,
   But when was that to me?

But now the world is older,
   And now to-morrow's come.
The winds are rushing colder,
   And all the birds are dumb.
And icy shackles fetter
   The brooklet's sunny blue—
And I was never better;
   But what is that to you?

SONG FOR AN APRIL DUSK

Tell me tales of a lilied pool
    Asleep beneath the sun.
Tell me of woodlands deep and cool,
    When chuckling satyrs run.
Tell me, in light and tinkling words,
    Of rippling, lilting streams.
Tell me of radiant-breasted birds,
    Who sing their amorous dreams.
Tell of the doomed butterfly
    That flings his hour away.
Fated to live and love and die
    Before the death of day.

Tell me tales of the moon-pale sprites
    Whose beauty none may know.
Tell me of secret, silver nights
    When great red stars are low.
Tell of the virgin Spring, the fair,
    Who roams the circling years.
Rain-drops strung in her fragrant hair,
    Her eyes a-mist with tears.
Tell me of elves, who leap to kiss,
    Who trip the velvet sward.
Tell me stories of things like this,
    And, boy, will I be bored!

ROSEMARY [2]

I wear your fragrant memory, like a spray of mignonette,
    As I tread the winding ribbon of the years.
How clear the radiant image of you stands before me yet
    In the thousand little mirrors of my tears.
And ah, my dearest love, when I forget the way to dream
    I'll forget your silent nearness in the dark,
Where languorous lilies floated on a quiet woodland stream—
    Or were you the one I'd meet in Central Park?
The love of you was sudden and the heart of you was strong;
    There were leaping little devils in your eyes;
Your laughter rode the morning like a joyous May-day song—
    No, I guess that must have been two other guys.

Could I forget your April smile, the shining way of you,
    Could I forget your method so adroit?
Could I forget those stories of the other girls you knew?
    Or was that the butter-and-egg man from Detroit?
A pair of truant children, we would often steal away
    Where the city's voice was gloriously mute,
And plan the little cottage we should have, one happy day—
    Or were you the boy that had the wife in Butte?
You had my first, my golden love, and though we're torn apart,
    Through all the circling years, I've been the same.
Your name is ever written on the pages of my heart—
    And, by the way, my dear, what *was* your name?

BALLADE OF A COMPLETE FLOP

Sad the matter of which I speak,
  Deep the trouble of which I sigh.
To the heavens my woes I shriek—
  I'd just love to sit down and cry.
  Though I hate to admit it, my
Batting av'rage is less than fair.
  Generous gentlemen pass me by—
All that they give me is the air.

Rich man, beggarman, merchant, sheik,
  Actor, congressman, human fly.
Argentinean, Czech, and Greek
  Give and give, till the well runs dry,
  Gifts of elderly Scotch and rye.
Gifts of jewels and orchids rare
  To a more competent Lorelei—
All that they give me is the air.

What's the matter with my technique?
  I can't fathom, or even try.
I'm intelligent, fond, and weak—
  Why don't I get a regular guy?
  Just for others, the goose hangs high;
All love's tokens that form my share
  May be placed in a pig's left eye—
All that they give me is the air.

L'Envoi
Princes, tell me the reason why.
　　What's the trouble, and how, and where?
When did Santa Claus go and die?
　　All that they give me is the air.

FOLK SONG

Robin, he is strong and sure,
   Gallant, wise, and gay.
Gavin's heart is calm and pure
   As the new-born day.
Steady shine young Alan's eyes,
   Deep with honesty.
Jack, he tells me naught but lies—
   He's the lad for me.

Richard vows no other maid
   Did he love before.
Will, his beating heart he laid
   At my cottage door.
Peter tells me, "None but you
   Am I thinking of."
Jack, he's wondrously untrue—
   He's my own dear love.

Casper's hair is golden brown;
   Hal is straight and slim.
Martin's richest in the town—
   Who'd say "no" to him?
Rafe's a fine young gentleman;
   Tom's with virtue blest.
Jack, he broke my heart and ran—
   I love him the best.

COLLEGE BOYS

A HYMN OF HATE

I hate College Boys;
They get under my feet.

There are the Boy Butterflies;
The Haberdashers' Livelihood.
Society would be on the rocks without them;
They are as much a part of every tea
As the watercress sandwiches.
They list all the débutantes
In Grades A, B, and C,
And proceed accordingly.
Once they get into their stride,
The Opposite Sex hasn't a prayer.
They are great boys in the moonlight,
And if there were ever a contest in sitting out dances
They could enter at scratch.
They are always dropping lavender envelopes,
Or returning photographs,
Or leaving word that they are not at home
In case a woman's voice asks for them on the telephone.
They wish to God the girls would leave them alone—
That falls right in with my plans.

Then there are the Athletes;
All Full of Red Blood, or What Have You?
They eat their meat just this side of raw,
They are constantly flinging windows open,
And they can hardly wrench themselves out of their cold showers.

They may be the Biceps Kings,
But if you sneak up on them suddenly,
And ask them who discovered America,
They have to rack their memories.
They are all due to make a big name in the business world;
Look at the way they can tear telephone books in half,
And bend silver quarters,
And chin themselves seventy-five consecutive times.
When football comes into the conversation,
It turns out that they are the boys who wrote the rules.
They are always doing something helpful—
You find them on the bathing beaches
Forming human pyramids;
Or on country club verandas
Holding rocking-chairs out at arm's length;
Or standing on their hands
In some lucky girl's parlor.
It's rough that they have to be cramped up in cities;
Way up in the clean, cold, silent out-of-doors,
That's where they ought to be—
And now!

There are the Hot Puppies;
The High-Place Hitters.
They may be young as years go,
But they are old in night life.

You would never dream of the wicked things that go on
If they didn't take pity
And clear it all up for you.
They have piled up a nasty record for themselves;
Try and hear it without blushing.
They tear the town wide open
Until nearly eleven o'clock at night,
They talk right back to policemen.
And when it comes to alcohol,
They imply that they can take it or let it alone—
Reading from left to right.
They concede that they are just about as scarlet as they come,
And they perform a mean laugh,
And say that terrible isn't the word for them—
I heard different.

And there are the Heavy Thinkers;
The Boys That Know the Answers.
Bring up any subject at all
And they'll be glad to set you right on it.
I forget what they go to college for:
It can't be education,
Because they had all that under control years ago.
They don't go so big on a dance floor,
But when the party gets loose,
And Greek irregular verbs are being bandied about,
They are the hit of the evening.
They can hold their audiences spellbound;
If it isn't the latest trigonometry problem that's going the rounds,

Then it's the good one the boys are telling
About the advantages of the parliamentary form of government.
If they were to appear in public
Without a book under their arm
They would feel as if they had come out without their socks.
They seldom hear, when they are spoken to;
It's because their heads are so full
Of little gems of old-world philosophy—
You know the old crack:
Nietzsche abhors a vacuum.

I hate College Boys;
They get under my feet.

BALTO

*(THE LEAD DOG OF THE TEAM
THAT BROUGHT ANTITOXIN TO NOME)*

I think that you could only pity me
    Who'd want to weep and stroke your head and coo
And murmur little names, mellifluously,
    And know no other thing to do.

What should I do, but drop my eyes, and strain
    To cloak the meanness of my offerings,
Who am aggrieved at cold, and hide from pain,
    And live with little, little things.

My days slip by in thin and wavering line;
    Softened my life to such as sick men lead.
And sharp there cuts across dimmed hours like mine
    The cold white radiance of your deed.

Outraging cornered Death, you held the course
    Against the whining night, the whirling day.
When man gave over to the inhuman force,
    Then it was you who led the way.

Though never trumpet urged you to the fight,
    And roystering rush of war was not your part,
Your spirit was a rocket in the night,
    You bore a banner in your heart.

Not hope of cited glory led you then,
    Simply, so went your days since they began.
You did the thing, nor thought of it again,
    A very gallant gentleman.

CASSANDRA DROPS INTO VERSE

We'd break the city's unfeeling clutch
   And back to good Mother Earth we'd go,
With birds and blossoms and such-and-such,
   And love and kisses and so-and-so.
We'd build a bungalow, white and green,
   With rows of hollyhocks, all sedate.
And you'd come out on the five-eighteen
   And meet me down at the garden gate.

We'd leave the city completely flat
   And dwell with chickens and cows and bees,
'Mid brooks and bowers and this and that,
   And joys and blisses and those and these.
We'd greet together the golden days,
   And hail the sun in the morning sky.
We'd find an Eden—to coin a phrase—
   The sole inhabitants, you and I.

With sweet simplicity all our aim,
   We'd fare together to start anew
In peace and quiet and what's-its-name,
   And soul communion, or what have you?
But oh, my love, if we made the flight,
   I see the end of our pastoral plan. . . .
Why, you'd be staying in town each night,
   And I'd elope with the furnace man.

MEETING-PLACE

Here the sky is clear and deep—
    Tedious heart, be gay, be gay!
One and one, like counted sheep,
    Clouds go gamboling away.
(Mary, robed in white and blue,
    Let him swear he has been true.)

Here the leaves are cool and slow—
    Then be quiet, shrieking mind!
And the gracious boughs are low,
    And the roots are sure and kind.
(Lord, that died upon a tree,
    Let him lie, and comfort me.)

SONG OF AMERICANS RESIDENT IN FRANCE

Oh, we are the bold expatriate band!
Allegiance we vow to our chosen land.
How gladly we'd offer our all to France.
We'd give her our honor, our souls, our pants.
We hail her the highest of earthly heavens;
We wriggle our shoulders, and cross our 7's.
With tolerant laughter we rock and sway
Whenever we think of the U.S.A.
At Yankee behavior we writhe and blench.
Our English is rusty—we think in French.
The Sorrows of France disarrange our sleep;
With Gallic abandon we bleed, we weep.
We long to lay down for her all we have;
We love her, we love her, *la belle, la brave!*
We'd see given back to her all her due—
The grandeur, the glory that once she knew.
We'd have her triumphantly hung with flowers,
Acknowledged supremest of all the Powers,
Her dominance written in white and black . . .
But, boy, we'd be sore if the franc came back!

RHYME OF AN INVOLUNTARY VIOLET

When I ponder lovely ladies
Slipping sweetly down to Hades,
Hung and draped with glittering booty—
Am I distant, cold and snooty?
Though I know the price their pearls are
Am I holier than the girls are?
Though they're lavish with their "Yes's,"
Do I point, and shake my tresses?
No! I'm filled with awe and wonder.
I review my every blunder . . .
Do I have the skill to tease a
Guy for an Hispano-Suiza?
I can't even get me taxis
Off to Sydneys, Abes, and Maxies!
Do the pretty things I utter
To the kings of eggs and butter
Gain me pearls as big as boulders,
Clattering, clanking round my shoulders,
Advertising, thus, their full worth?
No, my dear, Mine come from Woolworth.
Does my smile across a table
Win a cloak of Russian sable?
Baby, no. I'd have to kill a
Man to get a near-chinchilla.
Men that come on for conventions
Show me brotherly intentions;
Though my glance be fond and melting,
Do they ever start unbelting
With the gifts they give the others?

No! They tell me of their mothers,
To the baby's pictures treat me,
Say they want the wife to meet me!
Gladly I'd be led to slaughter
Where the ermine flows like water,
When the gay white globes are lighted;
But I've never been invited!
So my summary, in fact, is
What an awful flop my act is!

THE TEMPTRESS

You'd think, with all the age and sense
It has by now, that Providence
Would overlook my vaporings,
And turn its mind to bigger things.
You'd think, compared with flood and war,
My small concerns would be a bore.
But no! The world may go to pot
While I have service no one got.
For do I stretch myself, and smile,
And bask in peace a little while,
And rashly murmur, "Here is bliss"—
It cries, "We must look into this!
Too full her cup to bear a drop;
Well, well, this thing has got to stop."
Or do I weep me harsh and dry,
And raise my futile fists on high,
And curse my dam, and sob, and sweat—
It says, "She ain't seen nothing yet"
(Considering this the latest slang).
So letting all the world go hang,
It sets itself to showing me
What true unhappiness may be.
Ah, could I tempt assorted gents
As sure as I can Providence,
A different story I'd rehearse,
And damned if I'd be writing verse!

TO ELSPETH

Lady, I have read your verse on
Me—the one wherein you write
"How I'd like to meet that person
All alone some ebon night!"

Though your wish to wound were little,
You have done your worst—you see,
Some one, when my heart was brittle,
Said those very words to me.

Lady, take my humble greetings;
Take my thanks; but let me say
Were it not for midnight meetings,
I'd be on my feet to-day.

WHEN WE WERE VERY SORE

(LINES ON DISCOVERING THAT YOU HAVE BEEN ADVERTISED
AS AMERICA'S A. A. MILNE.)

Dotty had
Great Big
Visions of
Quietude.
Dotty saw an
Ad, and it
Left her
Flat.
Dotty had a
Great Big
Snifter of
Cyanide.
And that (said Dotty)
Is that.

THE ACCURSED

Oh, I shall be, till Gabriel's trump,
Nostalgic for some distant dump;
And ever doomed to weep me dry
For some lost mediocre guy.

CHRIS-CROSS

ON CONFUSING MESSRS. MORLEY AND ROBIN

Christopher Morley goes hippetty, hoppetty,
Hippetty, hippetty, hop.
Whenever I ask him politely to stop it, he
Says he can't possibly stop. . . .

GRANDE PASSION

If you should break your beauteous nose,
My love would perish, I suppose;
Or did your hair go limp and straight,
I might again be celibate.
Were you to slide your step, and peer,
You'd see my little back, I fear;
But lose, my love, your soul and sense—
I should not know the difference.

EXCURSION INTO ASSONANCE

I have trodden level sand
    Along a reach of gray—
From dune-top to sea's end,
    No breathing thing but me.

I have dropped the heavy latch
    Against the rain's tap,
And shivered by the fire, to watch
    The dark hours slip.

The desolate beach, the midnight storm—
    I dwelt alone with these;
But here, within your bended arm,
    Is loneliness.

—AND RETURN

I walked upon a vacant shore
    Beneath a low and thickening sky;
I faced the empty sea, and swore,
    "There is no lonelier one than I."

I waited through a night of lead;
    I heard the showers slide and hiss,
And started at my voice, that said,
    "No loneliness has been but this."

But here, my heart against your own,
    Your petulant kiss to silence me,
I know that I had never known
    How bitter lonely I could be.

SONG OF SOCIAL LIFE IN HOLLYWOOD

One speculates—or doesn't one?
Upon our movie actors' fun;
For it is true as it is right
They don't make pictures all the night.
Now what can there be left, to please
Such fortunates, in hours of ease?
Who labors for his daily bread
Rehearsing scenes would knock you dead
'Mid groves designed, as if by fairies,
For love, and its subsidiaries,
And every lithe and gifted hero
Makes whoopee, *à la mode de* Nero,
With women, wine, and even song,
The livelong day, the live day long—
What's his for fun, when work is through?
What can he do, what DOES he do?
Oh, ask me that, for I have found
There is a rule the world around;
The busman, in his hours of play,
Doth ride a bus, for holiday.

SONNET [2]

In seemly burial, love may not rest;
   A newer love must come to bear away
   The unwanted body of the dead, and lay
The wraith that stalks the heart, a tedious guest.
Let them that knew no fullness go protest
   Their vacant hearts; thus boldly may they say
   That know not haunted night and troubled day.
None who has loved bears now an empty breast.

Weary and waiting, ever on and on,
   Cold love, uncoffined, walks its rut of woe;
Only the live can bid the dead begone—
   The new must come, before the old may go.
And they alone may end the mournful tale
And cry "Farewell" who first have uttered "Hail!"

LETTER TO OGDEN NASH

CHALET LA BRUYERE, MONTANA-VERMALA, SWITZERLAND

Dear Sir, I trust you will pardon this intrusion of an Old
    Subscriber
Who used to dabble for a living in rhyme, as well as vers libre,
But has now Got Away From It All, owing to a plethora of
    intellectuals,
Racquet Club members, players on two pianos, raconteurs, and
    homosectuals.
I want very much to tell you that were you on an Alp, as I'm,
You would get Ogden Nash's verses though you had to commit
    arson or m'hy'm.
I little thought, at my time of life, to be anxiously awaiting the
    New Yorker,
(Although I do not buy it, but borrow my friends', thus
    contributing nothing to the stockholders' exchorquer)
But now it's my whitest hope, for I think you are considerably
    greater
Than Walter Savage Landor, Walter de la Mare, Walter Winchell,
    and Walter Pater,
I wish you all successes, in life as in lit'rature,
And I remain your respectful admirer from the very bottom of
    my coeur.

AFTER DAWN

Theodore Dreiser
Should ought to write nicer.

SONG IN THE WORST POSSIBLE TASTE
FOR A CERTAIN MR. S., WHO GOT PERSONAL

I shall not see—and don't I know 'em?
A critic lovely as a poem.

OUR COUSINS

Ever I view those people dumbly
Surnamed Mainwaring or Cholmondeley;
Folk at home my sapience staggers
Schooled at Magdalen or Jesus.
Never have I ascertained
Why they all are so refined—
Why aloofness sheds its spell
On the littlest boy or girl—
Why they're stiffer than a bible
On a solid oaken table.
Though I puzzle, make no head I can—
That's for being un-American.

THE PASSIONATE SCREEN WRITER
TO HIS LOVE

Oh come, my love, and join with me
The oldest infant industry.
Come seek the bourne of palm and pearl,
The lovely land of Boy-Meets-Girl,
Come grace this lotus-laden shore,
This Isle of Do-What's-Done-Before.
Come, curb the new, and watch the old win,
Out where the streets are paved with Goldwyn.

THREAT TO A FICKLE LADY

Sweet Lady Sleep, befriend me;
    In pretty mercy, hark.
Your charming manners, tend me—
    Let down your lovely dark.

Sweet lady, take me to you,
    Becalm mine eyes, my breath. . . .
Remember, I that woo you
    Have but to smile at Death. . . .

INDEX OF TITLES AND FIRST LINES